The S

CONTENTS

Martin Simons is a retired Civil Engineer. He was born in Bromley, Kent, and raised in South East London, where a 360 acre park 'playground', literally over the back fence, nurtured an affinity with nature in the suburbs.

Martin moved to the Sussex Coast, where he lives, near both beach and Downs, with his wife, Gilly. Their four children have fled the nest, two internationally to Mexico and Tenerife, one to London, as a TV presenter, and one locally. Martin's treasured first grandchild, Tonito, lives in Mexico, but the second is to be born and bred in Sussex!

For many years, Martin was involved in girls' and women's football, managing cup and championship winning teams with Brighton and Hove Albion.

Walking the Downs succeeded football as a dominant leisure activity, which soon matured into a passion –and then a mission! Existing walking guides consistently failed to impress, and were judged to be lacking in both accuracy and imagination. Martin was soon poring over OS Explorer maps, meticulously planning and recording the very best walking routes on the South Downs. This book is the culmination of his endeavours.

ACKNOWLEDGEMENTS

My wife, Gilly, has encouraged and supported me, her female sense of direction crucial in testing the walks. Dave Sargent and Jo Hind have been my main testers, with Jo's editorial advice proving invaluable. And finally, thanks to David and Ros Brawn for putting the whole thing together and guiding me through the technicalities of the early days.

One summer's evening I was climbing a shady woodland path up a steep scarp slope near **Storrington**. As I stopped for a breather, I could hear footsteps behind me, but could see not a soul! Slightly spooked, as dusk started to fall, I quickened my pace until, gasping for air, I stopped again - the footsteps were louder! Imagination ran wild, primeval fears surfaced; then realization dawned! The footsteps were the thumping of my own pounding heart in the silent twilight! Just goes to show that walking on the South Downs is not a stroll in the park, but often as lung-busting as any range of hills in England.

A staggeringly beautiful and varied landscape, changing with the seasons, the South Downs offers formidable scarp slopes, towering cliffs, flowing contours, river valleys, and a wealth of woodland. Rich in history: prehistoric burial mounds, Iron Age hill forts, ancient tucked away churches, attractive villages and inns, all set in a backdrop of rolling undulating hills.

With challenging climbs, the rewards are, at times, jaw-dropping! Nearly 2000 miles of footpaths and bridleways crisscross the Downs, as well as new paths across access land and nature reserves, stretching the 80 miles from **Eastbourne** to **Winchester**. On many of the walks you may hardly see a soul, for despite the proximity of large populations, getting away from it all is a welcome reality.

CREATION OF THE DOWNS

100 to 75 million years ago, Southern Britain was covered by a 500 metre deep sea. Microscopic algae were eaten by tiny shrimp-like creatures, and their excrement sank to the sea bed; hence there's the slightly startling probability that chalk derives from shrimp droppings! You could imagine that the sea was a cloudy white soup; in fact, the chalk formed very slowly - in a human lifetime of, say, 75 years, only one millimetre of ooze would have been formed. The bands of flint visible in cliffs, quarries, and sometimes liberally scattered over arable fields, are organic in origin, probably from decaying matter gathered in the burrows of scavenging creatures on the sea floor.

Cliff erosion near Newhaven

The chalk-producing process stopped as the seas became warmer and shallower, a younger deposit of softer material being deposited 55 to 45 million years ago on top of the chalk. This layer has been almost completely weathered away, with the exception of some outcrops in the Solent area, and the larger sarsen stones, particularly evident in **Stanmer Park** near **Brighton**.

As the earth's crust heaved and buckled, pressure from the African continent folded and lifted the chalk bed as it pushed against Europe. Weathering and rivers cut into the chalk until, 2 million to 14,000 years ago, water from thawing snow and ice carved valleys into the frozen chalk, forming many of the dry valleys we see today. The softer chalk was eroded away. All that remains today are the north and south edges, now the North Downs and the South Downs, separated by the Weald. The erosion of the south edge of the Downs continues today - the sea of the English Channel nibbling inexorably away; see the photo on the previous page.

MAN ON THE DOWNS

The earliest appearance of man was an astonishing 500,000 years ago, on the dip slope of the Downs at **Boxgrove**. Only during warmer phases of the Ice Ages could nomadic hunters roam. Around 12,000 years ago, as the tundra thawed, the bare landscape very slowly transformed as trees became established. Wild animals moved north, crossing the land bridge which joined England with what is now France, and fish became abundant in rivers. The supply of food brought the hunter gatherers, followed by the first herder farmers of the Neolithic Age (5000–1500BC), with clearance of trees from the thin downland soil being easier than anywhere else. This was the start of sheep and dung farming - the dung from the sheep, penned in overnight, providing nutrients to the poor soil to enable crops to be grown - a system which endured into the 20th century. The Neolithic farmers left relatively few marks on the landscape, the most notable being the long barrow burial mounds, containing up to 50 bodies. There are a number of enclosures bound by ditches, not thought to have been fortifications, but possibly used as meeting places, or communal lambing enclosures, as protection against the ravages of wolves. It was the Neolithic Age that saw the earliest manufacturing industry - flint tools - the raw flint being mined at **Blackpatch** and **Church Hill**, near **Findon**, both dated to 4,000 BC. Other mines were at **Harrow Hill**, **Bow Hill**, **Windover Hill** and, biggest of all, **Cissbury Ring**.

From the late Neolithic into the Bronze Age (1500–500BC) one of the commonest features of the high Downs is the round barrow, denoted on OS maps as tumuli or tumulus.

They contained cremated remains in a pottery container, the two main types being the bell barrow (the mound is surrounded by a flat area then a ditch), and the bowl barrow (the mound is closely bound by a ditch). Most were robbed by 18th and 19th century 'treasure' seekers.

Sussex Archaeology Society with Sussex University: archaeological dig of a Bronze Age hut platform alongside the Green Way (Walk 7)

The Iron Age (500BC–64AD) saw the construction of hill forts, a major feature of the Downs today. By 100BC there was a series of forts covering the entire range. By 100AD, the woodland was probably entirely cleared and the Downs had a dense population - more than any other time in history. Romano-British (64 -450AD) fields covered large areas, as evidenced by the number of field boundaries still visible today, despite extensive bulldozing for food production during the last war. In contrast, the Weald was almost uninhabited, due to the heavy soil and dense impassable forest. There are few Roman features on the Downs. A number of bridleways have their origins as minor Roman roads - only **Stane Street** from **Bignor Hill** towards **Chichester** is well preserved.

With the demise of the Roman presence, the Dark Ages began (450–1066AD). The Saxons invaded and became the controlling power. There are few remains from this period except for a number of Saxon features in some churches, and forts built around the time of King Alfred on all the rivers of the Downs, probably as protection against Danish raiders.

Sussex Archaelogy Society with Sussex University dig of a 9th / 10th century Saxon settlement alongside Bishopstone Church (Walk 6)

With the Norman invasion of 1066, castles appeared at **Lewes**, **Bramber**, and **Arundel**. Several motte and bailey fortifications, and many of the downland churches we see today, were also built.

CHURCHES

Almost every walk passes near to a church. They vary between amazing and dull, so I've been quite selective about those mentioned in the text. Make your own judgment by visiting as many as you wish; a small donation towards upkeep would be appreciated.

All Medieval churches, from the 11th to the 15th centuries, had wall paintings, some of which survive today. There were no books to teach Christianity to the masses, so the wall paintings illustrated stories from the Bible - a teaching aid. However, they were lime-washed over, by order, in 1547, as they were thought to be popish! Many Medieval fonts were kept padlocked, to prevent witches from stealing the Holy water!

Adam and Eve wall painting, Hardham Church, 1130AD (Walk 29)

Sometimes the comment, "The Victorians have ruined this church," is heard. Before criticizing their renovations, bear in mind that, when Victoria came to the throne, religion was totally out of fashion. Churches were in a deplorable state, many almost complete ruins. So the Victorian 're-builds' probably saved many churches from disappearing altogether.

A wide variety of habitats exist on and around the Downs. 13% are Sites of Special Scientific Interest and nature conservation, 22% is covered in a wide range of woodland, and only 3% is unimproved grass chalkland (organic meadow). There's a wealth of wild flowers: primrose, celandine, wood anemone, bluebell, and the distinctive garlic aroma of the ramson - all common in spring woodland. The arrival of summer is heralded by the red campion, adorning woodland edges, and the majestic foxglove in woodland clearings. The open downland has displays of cowslips, pyramid orchids, bird's-foot trefoil. In fact, up to 40 different plants can be found in a square yard of turf, and the sweet smell of herbs bruised underfoot is always a delight.

Marbled White butterfly (Walk 8)

This range of plants attracts a variety of butterflies, from the first flights of brimstones and orange tips, the early summer marbled white and the beautiful blues, to the occasional continental invasion of the clouded

yellow in late summer. A good butterfly identification book is a 'must', to appreciate the number of species, ever changing as spring progresses to autumn.

Large Skipper butterfly (Walk 8)

Birds you are almost guaranteed to hear on any walk include the laughing cackle of the green woodpecker, the clattering wings of the wood pigeon, the raucous croak of the pheasant, and occasionally the whirring wings of the partridge. Not so long ago, to see or hear a buzzard was a rare occurrence. Now, they are almost common, with their distinctive mewing call, particularly in the western Downs. On the open Downs the skylark still reigns supreme, and the wheatear, once so common that shepherds earned extra income trapping it in turf traps in its thousands for London gourmets, puts in a late summer appearance. There's an old Sussex saying, "Wen yuz sees a whole lotta crows together, then theys rooks, an when yuz sees a rook by isself, then ee´s a crow." Having spent the last year testing this theory, the conclusion is - twaddle!

The character of the Downs gradually changes from east to west, with trees of all types, including Europe's largest yew forest, becoming increasingly concentrated. Although deer can be seen at the eastern end, it is the more densely wooded west where they are most common. To be startled by a herd of deer bursting across a woodland path is an unforgettable experience. Even at a distance it's a thrill, with the occasional view of a white deer always possible.

If you're lucky you may see an adder basking in the sun, and there's a fair chance you may see a fox running across a field. Voles and shrews are common, with their high pitched squeaks; unlike children, they are heard and not seen. Rabbits can be seen in their hundreds in some places, and there are a surprising number of badgers' sets, although you will probably have to be nocturnal to spot one. But perhaps the biggest delight is to see a hare at close quarters - a truly beautiful mammal.

The ancient yew grove, Kingley Vale (Walk 36)

THE WALKS

The walks in this book are the best the Downs can offer. Every one has something special - all have an element of wow-factor! Each walk has been thoroughly researched and independently tested (without a map), to ensure accurate and, dare I say it, foolproof directions. For GPS converts, precise, easily downloadable, routes from the Discovery Walking Guides PNF CD can be used in association with this book.

The walks can be started at any point where parking can be found, to fit personal preferences regarding refreshments. If you are going to park in a pub car park, please seek permission first (pub phone numbers are in Appendix A), and leave a note on the windscreen.

I've tried to avoid routes near unacceptably noisy major roads, and also bridleways that are churned to a quagmire by horses.

GPS signals are good on all routes, although there will be the occasional odd spot where a dense leaf canopy shields signals in summer.

The timings between waypoints serve as a guide only. We all walk at varying speeds, and I've not included stops to admire views etc.

I've deliberately avoided the use of the term 'way post', using marker post instead, to avoid confusion with waypoints. Finally, before you venture forth into this amazing landscape, a word on access land. We all welcome the opportunity to walk on new land, but be aware that landowners may restrict access rights for 28 days a year for any reason. (see www.countrysideaccess.gov.uk).

Marker post overlooking Edburton Church (Walk 20)

A good pair of boots is the best investment you can make. I wear Brasher Hillmasters - still going strong after 10 years, teamed up with a pair of quality walking socks. A 'grippy' sole is essential to cope with slippery scarp slopes (wet chalk can be like walking on ice), and dry, crumbly slopes are equally hazardous. Be aware that, if you venture into the Weald, the going may be heavy and soggy. Gaiters may be a useful addition, particularly in winter.

Being of a frugal disposition, I wear what I find comfortable and affordable. My apparel is based on thin layers under a zip-up fleece jacket, multi-pocketed trousers, and a seasonal hat (essential for the follicly challenged like me). Even when the ground is frozen, once walking and climbing, I find I am self-heating. The only coat I wear is a pouch-sized breathable waterproof, donned if necessary, to keep out wind and rain. Extreme weather is unusual on the Downs, unless you are a glutton for punishment and go looking for it, and I like to walk with minimum clutter. A small rucksack with water, waterproofs, chocolate and a banana, sunscreen, lip salve, elastoplast, small binoculars, spare GPS batteries, a whistle if on my own, a compass that I have never yet had occasion to use, and a mobile phone with a fully charged battery (note that mobile phones do not work in some areas).

Warm summer days encourage the wearing of shorts, though nettles can be a problem. The answer is to carry a small pair of secateurs to cut and trim a suitable beating stick, then thrash them into submission!

One final tip: picture the scene as you arrive at a pub with wet and muddy boots. You soil your hands taking them off to leave outside, then worry that someone is going to steal them leaving you stranded in your socks! A pair of Tesco carrier bags is the perfect remedy. Put your foot in, tie the handles together and away you go. Perhaps not for the fashion icons among you, but it certainly works!

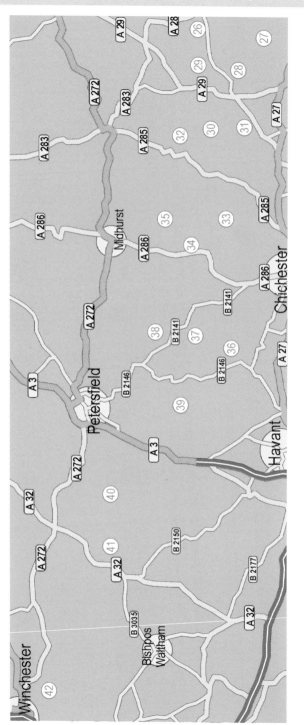

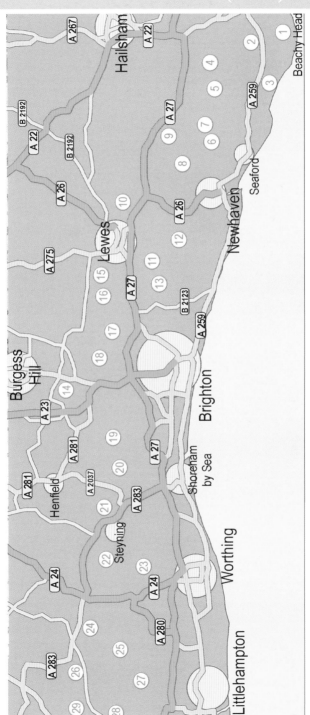

our rating for effort/exertion:-
1 very easy **2** easy **3** average
4 energetic **5** strenuous

 approximate **time** to complete a walk (compare your times against ours early in a walk) - does not include stopping time

 approximate walking **distance** in miles/kilometres

 approximate **ascents/descents** in metres (N=negligible)

circular route

linear route

figure of eight route

risk of **vertigo**

 refreshments rated **1-5** (may be at start or end of a route only)

Walk descriptions include:
● timing in minutes, shown as (40M)
● compass directions, shown as (NW)
● GPS waypoints, shown as (Wp.3)

Notes on the text
Place names are shown in **bold text**, except where we refer to a written sign, when they are enclosed in single quotation marks. Local or unusual words are shown in *italics*, and are explained in the accompanying text.

All the map sections which accompany the detailed walk descriptions in Walk! The South Downs are reproduced under Ordnance Survey licence from the digital versions of the latest Explorer 1:25,000 scale maps. Each map section is then re-scaled to the 40,000 scale used in DWG's Walk!/Walks series of guide books. Walking Route and GPS Waypoints are then drawn onto the map section to produce the map illustrating the detailed walk description.

Walk! The South Downs map sections are sufficient to follow the detailed walk descriptions, but for planning your adventures in this region we strongly recommend that you purchase the latest OS Explorer maps.

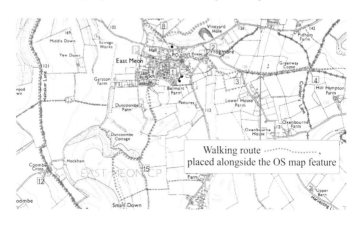

Walking route ....,
placed alongside the OS map feature

The GPS Waypoint lists provided in this book are as recorded by Martin Simons while researching the detailed walk descriptions. Waypoint symbols are numbered so that they can be directly identified with the walk description and waypoint list. All GPS Waypoints are subject to the accuracy of GPS units in the particular location of each waypoint.

In the beautiful landscapes of the South Downs, GPS reception is excellent for the majority of Martin's walking routes, the exception being the occasional odd spot where a very dense leaf canopy shields signals in summer.

Satellite Reception
Accurate location fixes for your GPS unit depend upon you receiving signals from four or more satellites. Providing you have good batteries, and that you wait until your gps has full 'satellite acquisition' before starting out, your gps will perform well on the South Downs.

Manually Inputting Waypoints
GPS Waypoints are quoted for the OSGB (Ordnance Survey Great Britain) datum and BNG (British National Grid) coordinates, making them identical with the OS grid coordinates of the position they refer to. To manually input the Waypoints into your GPS we suggest that you:

- switch on your GPS and select 'simulator/standby' mode
- check that your GPS is set to the OSGB datum and BNG 'location/position format'
- input the GPS Waypoints into a 'route' with the same number as the walking route; then when you call up the 'route' on the South Downs there will be no confusion as to which walking route it refers
- repeat the inputting of waypoints into routes until you have covered all the routes you plan to walk, or until you have used up the memory capacity of your GPS
- turn off your GPS. When you turn your GPS back on it should return to its normal navigation mode.

Note that GPS Waypoints complement the routes in Walk! The South Downs, and are not intended as an alternative to the detailed walking route descriptions.

Personal Navigator Files (PNFs) CD
Edited versions of Martin Simons' original GPS research tracks and waypoints are available as downloadable files on our PNFs CD, which also includes all the edited GPS tracks and waypoints for all the Walk!/Walks guide books published by DWG along with GPS Utility Special Edition software. See DWG websites for more information
> www.walking.demon.co.uk & www.dwgwalking.co.uk

GPS The Easy Way (£4.99)
If you are confused by talk of GPS, but are interested in how this modern navigational aid could enhance your walking enjoyment, then simply seek out a copy of GPS The Easy Way, the UK's best selling GPS manual.

Well, two lighthouses actually! Where the **South Downs** meet the sea near **Eastbourne** is the classic **Beachy Head** cliff top walk.

The **Belle Tout Lighthouse** was first lit in 1834 by thirty oil lamps in an attempt to stem the number of shipwrecks on this stretch of coast. It met with limited success as the lighthouse was often obscured by sea fog, so in 1902 was replaced, two miles east, by the red and white lighthouse in the sea below **Beachy Head**. In 1999 the **Belle Tout Lighthouse**, now a private residence, was moved back from the cliff edge to stop it falling into the sea.

It's a pretty spectacular coastline, popular all year round. By contrast, the return route inland is on quiet, grassy, downland paths away from the hustle and bustle around **Beachy Head** itself. A visit to the beach can be added at **Birling Gap** at the west end of the walk.

3 | 3H 10M | 7 miles/11.3km | 365m / 365m | 2

Access by car:
Free parking at the National Trust car park **Birling Gap** (entrance next to the red telephone box). There are a number of other car parks on or near the route, which are all pay and display with the exception of **Beachy Head Pub**.

Short Walk (A)
3 miles/4.8km (1¼ hours). Parking at **Birling Gap**, turning left at Wp.3, to rejoin route at Wp.16 for return to **Birling Gap**.

Short Walk (B)
5 miles/8km (2 hours 20 minutes), parking (pay and display) in vicinity of **Beachy Head Pub** to start the walk from the viewing point at Wp.6. We turn left at Wp.16 to arrive at the cliff top path at Wp.3, turning left for the return to **Beachy Head**.

We start from the car park entrance by the red telephone box (Wp.1 0M). Heading up the hill (E) away from Birling Gap, we climb towards **Belle Tout Lighthouse** on the cliff-top path. Passing the lighthouse on the landward side, we descend to a roadside car park by the cliff edge (Wp.2 18M) before climbing up the cliff top path towards **Beachy Head**. Peeking over the cliff top from time to time (vertigo sufferers beware), we are rewarded with views of the **Beachy Head Lighthouse** in the sea below.

For Short Walk (A) from **Birling Gap**, we turn left at a stone boundary post (Wp.3 35M) and follow a bridleway downhill and away from the sea, crossing the road and continuing to a crossroads with a footpath where we turn left (see Wp.16 below).

Beachy Head Lighthouse

Beachy Head is unfortunately, a favourite venue for suicides. Some years ago one desperate man drove his car over the top but as he was still wearing his seat belt he survived to be rescued. After recovering in hospital he bought himself a bike, came to Beachy Head, cycled over the edge, and made a proper job of it! I expect there's a moral to this story, but I'm not quite sure what!

After a while we come to an octagonal brick-built viewing point (Wp.4 55M). It's well worth reading the plaque on the north side, commemorating the part these Downs played in the Second World War.

Continuing along the top and ignoring a path descending on our right, we arrive at a smooth tarmac path (Wp.5 59M) near the **Beachy Head Pub**. We turn right, following the path down to a viewing point on the headland, surrounded by a low wooden fence (Wp.6 62M).

Three-quarters of the way round the viewing point, we step over the low fence (on a busy tourist day you may have to fight your way through throngs of people) onto a very steeply descending grassy path. Towards the bottom we come to a small sign 'Cliff Erosion - Path Diverted' (Wp.7 66M). We take the left fork. Continuing downhill, we come to a sign 'Danger Cliff Edge' opposite a bench inscribed 'Pause a while and muse' (Wp.8 69M). Here we turn left, going slightly uphill and away from the sea on a wide grassy path to come to a T-junction near a water trough (Wp.9 73M), where we turn right, following a wide grass track heading towards **Eastbourne**. The trees and bushes in this area attract many migrating birds, especially around **Whitebread Hole** above the playing field.

When we come to a fork in the track (Wp.10 97M) we ignore the right fork and keep ahead, going slightly uphill until we reach a largish tree on the right. In another 15 metres we turn left (Wp.11 102M), going steeply uphill away from the sea on a wide, grassy path.

Above Whitebread Hole near Wp.10

As we climb, we cross the **South Downs Way** and two further paths before reaching a junction of five grassy paths (Wp.12 115M). We turn left, with the **Beachy Head Pub** visible ahead in the distance. On the right hand side and at the edge of a road, we see a gate with two marker posts (Wp.13 119M).

We cross the road here, going up the access road to **Bullock Down Farm** to cross a stile on our left near a fingerpost (Wp.14. 121M). We head diagonally across the field on an indistinct grass footpath, gradually descending until eventually we reach a shallow valley floor.

Belle Tout Lighthouse

With **Belle Tout** ahead in the distance, we cross a stile (Wp.15 136M). Up on the hill to our right we can see a flint shepherd's hut and sheepfold, a remnant of the days when sheep reigned supreme on these Downs. We cross a stile, continuing down the valley until we reach a crossroads with a bridleway (Wp.16 151M) at another stile.

For Short Walk (B) with parking near **Beachy Head Pub**, we turn left here, following the bridleway across the road and on towards the sea, to join the cliff top path where we turn left to return to **Beachy Head** (see Wp.3 above).

Still heading towards **Belle Tout** and passing behind **Hodcombe Farm**, we come to a road (Wp.17 169M) which we cross, soon reaching a wide grass path where we turn right. This path takes us through a short stretch of woodland (Wp.18 176M). When **Birling Gap** comes into view we keep straight ahead to return to our start point (Wp.1 186M).

Perhaps a visit to the beach at **Birling Gap** for a picnic and a paddle (though not recommended in January!) or refreshments at the Hotel?

2 CRAPHAM BOTTOM

Atmospheric names abound on the Downs; **Bramble Bottom**, **Pea Down**, **Eldon Bottom**, **Crapham Down** and **Wigden's Bottom** are some we encounter on this walk. A rarity, virtually the whole walk is on grass! On open, rolling downland, west of **Eastbourne**, passing several dew ponds, we walk through classic sheep country. After climbing up the gentle slope of a beautiful tranquil valley, we come back to reality with a stretch of the **South Downs Way**, yielding panoramic views of **Eastbourne** and the coast to **Hastings** and beyond.

3 | 2H 10M | 6 miles/9.6km | 245m / 245m | 0

Access by Car

From the A259, west of **Eastbourne**, follow the signs for 'Seafront, Beachy Head'. In a little over half a mile, turn right into **Warren Hill** car park (pay and display). On entering the car park, turn right and park at the north-west end, near a bridleway gate by a steel field gate. Alternative parking (pay and display) in lay-by on the left, just past the car park entrance, if the main car park is closed in winter.

> **Short Walk**.
> At Wp.9 turn right to follow the bridleway up **Ringwood Bottom**. Re-join the route at Wp.15. (5 miles)

From the car park (Wp.1 0M) we pass through a bridleway gate next to a steel gate , to follow a grass track down to **Crapham Bottom**, with **Belle Tout Lighthouse** silhouetted against the sea in the far distance.

Reaching the floor of the valley, we go through a bridleway gate (Wp.2 11M) and continue descending on the track. Opting for the right hand of the two bridleway gates ahead (Wp.3 24M), we pass to the right of a working dew pond, a notice nearby describing the very personal service offered by South East Water.

south east water

East Hale Bottom Booster

0845 301 0845

The South East Water sign

We pass through another bridleway gate (Wp.4 17M) on a gentle descent down the attractive, lightly wooded, valley of **East Hale Bottom**. After passing another dew pond and a fairly tasteful water treatment works, cunningly disguised as a farm building, we go through a steel gate. In 17 yards we turn right through a bridleway gate (Wp.5 28M) to head up the hill, along the fence line and towards the distant flint buildings of **New Barn**. There are lots of buildings called 'New Barn' on the Downs; one thing you can be sure of, they're not new!

After a steady climb we go through a bridleway gate, taking time to look back at the view towards the sea before continuing on the track ahead. Passing **New**

Barn on our right, we turn right through another bridleway gate (Wp.6 37M) and head between a defunct dew pond and a flint shepherd's hut, the pond sadly superseded by a galvanized water trough. Passing the shepherd's hut, we follow the fence line to the corner of the field where we turn left (Wp.7 41M) and follow the fence line all the way down, noting the ancient field system banks on our left, before arriving at the road (Wp.8 53M).

Going through a bridleway gate, we cross the road carefully, go through another bridleway gate and follow the fingerpost direction for 'Willingdon Hill' on a barely discernible grass path. Dropping downhill, we head for and pass through a bridleway gate (Wp.9 56M), to the left of a lone house, then turn right onto a grass track. Almost immediately we come to another bridleway gate on our left.

For the slightly shorter walk
Follow this grass track up **Ringwood Bottom** to join with the **South Downs Way** at Wp.15.

We turn left through the bridleway gate, cross a tarmac road and go through a permissive bridleway gate to head down towards a fingerpost in the fence on our right where we cross a stile (Wp.10 59M), to head for **Pea Down**. We follow a faint, slightly sunken, footpath, up towards the crest of the hill to a stile (Wp.11 67M). Across the stile, we continue on a wide grassy path, following the line of a wire fence 10 yards to our right.

The lone wind-bent tree

Passing an old quarry pit on the left, we follow the rim to a lone wind-bent tree (Wp.12 78M). Just beyond the tree, we take a narrow path down through gorse bushes to a stile at the valley bottom (Wp.13 82M).

The narrow path at 82 minutes

Turning right to cross the stile and passing to the right of a marker post, we gradually bear right up the floor of **Eldon Bottom** until we cross a stile by a steel gate. A steady climb brings us to another stile (Wp.14 97M) at the junction with the **South Downs Way**. Laid out before us is the impressive view of the coastline from **Eastbourne** to **Hastings** and beyond.

Crossing the stile, we turn right following the **South Downs Way**. On reaching the golf course, we walk along the grass track to the right of the stony track. Arriving at a fingerpost (Wp.15 112M), by a concrete road coming up from **Ringwood Bottom**, we continue ahead and as we approach the A259 road, we keep to the right, following the stone track to the crossing point (Wp.16 117M). Carefully negotiating the road crossing, we walk up a short stretch of stone track to follow the very obvious main, wide, grass track.

At a fingerpost (Wp.17) we turn slightly right, signed 'Beachy Head', towards a round barrow with a somewhat disrespectful concrete trig point on top.

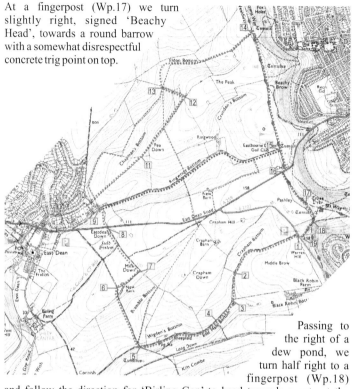

Passing to the right of a dew pond, we turn half right to a fingerpost (Wp.18) and follow the direction for 'Birling Gap' to head towards a gate at the roadside (Wp.19 126M), cross the road, enter the **Warren Hill** car park to return to our start (Wp.1 128M).

3 SEVEN SISTERS

One of the classic walks of the South Downs; forest, open rolling Downland, river valley, cliff top, and a very attractive village.

We start from the lovely village green of **East Dean**, passing **Friston Church** and through **Friston Forest**. We emerge into **Seven Sisters Country Park**, on beautiful paths with delightful views across the **Cuckmere Valley** before starting back over the **Seven Sisters** cliff tops. We return to **East Dean** from the south for welcome refreshment at the ancient **Tiger Inn**.

| 4 | 3H 5M | 8.2 miles/13.2km | 480m 480m | | 4 |

Access by car:
East Dean, west of **Eastbourne**, is off the A259. Follow the signs to the free village car park near **The Tiger Inn**.

Short Walk
A lovely short walk, a brief flirt with three of the **Sisters** before returning to **The Tiger Inn**. Follow the route to Wp.2, turn left before the kissing gate to follow the right fence line, pass through a bridleway gate maintaining direction to cross a stile onto a private road. Follow the road down through the hamlet of **Crowlink**, onto a bridleway down the valley bottom, eventually arriving at the cliff top to turn left at Wp.14. (1hour 25mins, 3.9 miles/6.3km)

Emerging from the car park we turn right, passing **The Tiger Inn** (Wp.1 0M) on the village green, looking forward to a pint on our return, as we most certainly will have earned it! Passing a row of cottages, we go through a flint wall, turning left along a road.

As the road bends left, we turn right up a concrete path, soon passing through a bridleway gate to follow a grass path up the middle of **Hobb's Eares**, a fine organic meadow.

Friston Church

At a kissing gate at the top (Wp.2 8M) (N.B. For the short walk, turn left before the gate), we go through, passing through two more closely spaced gates into the churchyard of the 11th century **Friston Church** which boasts a fine interior with a notable alabaster monument dated 1613, though a little unusual to find an ancient church with a fitted carpet!

We leave the churchyard through the Sussex speciality, a *tapsel* gate, crossing the road and turning right along the verge by a pond. We carefully cross the A259, on a path across a large grass traffic island, crossing a minor road to enter the fringes of **Friston Forest** by a footpath marker post (Wp.3 11M).

We soon turn right to drop down through the attractive woodland, go over a stile and diagonally cross a fine meadow on a grass path. In the far corner we leave over a stile, cross a road and climb steps to go through a kissing gate. Our path takes us across another pleasing meadow, passing through another kissing gate and crossing a road to immediately turn left by a marker post on a bridleway paralleling the road through a wood.

At a crossroads by a marker post (Wp.4 22M), we turn sharp left on a bridleway signed 'Westdene', soon joining the road we crossed earlier and following the left fence line. With **Friston Place** to our left, we keep ahead over a crossroads, eventually passing a 'neo-classical' waterworks, then a pair of cottages, as our road becomes an uphill track into the forest. At a T-junction we turn right, onto a wide terraced track (Wp.5 31M), ignoring the footpath which soon appears on our left. We pass through the forest, initially planted in 1918 to ensure that in future wars there would be an ample supply of timber as trench supports!

Just before two forest marker posts on our right, a left turn takes us up a steep, well-used footpath, unmarked but obvious (Wp.6 38M). Keeping an eye out for speeding cross country cyclists, we keep ahead over two forest tracks, to emerge at the A259 (Wp.7 45M). Crossing the road, we enter **Seven Sisters Country Park** through a kissing gate. Access to all areas is permitted in the park; however dogs must be kept on a lead during the lambing season. We keep ahead across a meadow, dropping down to a track, where we turn right to pass **Exceat New Barn**. Gently descending, we pass to the right of an isolated flint cottage, continuing down to the valley floor of **New Barn Bottom**. We go through a field gate on our left (Wp.8 52M), loosely following the right fence line on a grass track.

Eventually we turn right, crossing a stile (Wp.9 62M), making for, and crossing a stile on the skyline at the top of the hill (Wp.10 69M). Keeping ahead, we almost stumble over the stone marking the site of **Exceat Church**, probably destroyed by French raiders in the 15th century.

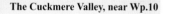
The Cuckmere Valley, near Wp.10

Cuckmere Haven, from near Wp.13

Still keeping ahead, fine views of the ox-bow lakes of the **River Cuckmere** open out as we drop down, bearing right to join a lovely grass, terraced path, descending to pass through a small temporary gate to a fingerpost by the park entrance (Wp.11 81M).

Here we have the option to cross the road to the **Seven Sisters Visitor Centre** or restaurant housed in a flint barn - well worth a visit. Maintaining direction, we pass a nearby fingerpost, turning left, through trees, at the fence by the car park entrance.

We emerge on a grass path, skirting the ox-bow lakes and along the edge of the wetland, eventually passing through a bridleway gate (Wp.12 99M) next to a field gate.

A flinty track takes us to a fingerpost, where we turn left, soon passing through another gate. Climbing steps, we follow the right fence line steadily uphill, with delightful views across **Cuckmere Haven** as we climb.

Crossing a stile, we follow the path up to a fingerpost (Wp.13 116M), bearing left (E) along the cliff top path across the first of the **Seven Sisters**, keeping away from the unfenced cliff edges.

A Fulmar patrols the cliffs (near Wp.14)

We tackle the ups and downs, until, crossing the second stile, we enter the **Crowlink** National Trust land by a sign. We drop down to the valley floor (Wp.14 138M), keeping ahead along the cliff top path.

Eventually, cresting the last summit, **Birling Gap** lies below, with **Belle Tout** lighthouse beyond. We descend to pass through a kissing gate and a footpath gate, soon turning left at a T-junction (Wp.15 162M). We go through two bridleway gates on a rising downland path, leaving the sea behind us as we head towards **East Dean**. Our track takes us towards a red barn; soon after passing it, as the track veers left, we bear half right to follow the right scrub line on a grass path which soon appears.

At a gap in the scrub overlooking the village below, we fork right (Wp.16 177M), down a 'hard to spot' terraced bridleway, descending through light woodland. We pass through a bridleway gate, crossing an organic meadow and leaving through a field gate.

We keep ahead on a tarmac road down through the village outskirts, crossing the green to the charming **Tiger Inn** (Wp.1 185M); for obvious reasons, it's very popular; and it also serves extremely good food!

4 THE LONG MAN OF WILMINGTON & BANOFEE PIE

The **Long Man of Wilmington** is the largest chalk hill human figure in Europe. He stands 240 feet tall and holds a long stave in each hand. His origins are a mystery, though the earliest record dates from 1710. He could be prehistoric, or the work of a monk from the nearby 13th century Benedictine priory with nothing better to do.

From the 13th century **Folkington Church**, on what was the main road between Eastbourne and Lewes in the days of coach and horses, we head west, passing below the **Long Man** before climbing **Windover Hill** with its marvellous views and a number of barrows. After crossing open downland we drop down to the village of **Jevington**, with the Banoffee Pie story; then back up the pretty **Willingdon Bottom** to visit a number of prehistoric features along the high north ridge, returning past **The Eight Bells** pub. The final leg takes us on a delightful footpath back to **Folkington**.

| 3 | 3H 25M | 8.5 miles/13.6km | ⛰ | 340m ↕ 340m | ↻ | 🍴 3 |

Short Walks
(A) 5.5 miles/8.8km (2 hours). From **Folkington** to the **Hungry Monk** at **Jevington** Wp.10, turn left along the village street to rejoin the route at **The Eight Bells** pub Wp.15.

(B) 3 miles/4.8km (1 ¼ hrs). Alternative parking at **Butts Brow** car park (pay and display), access via **Butts Lane** from **Willingdon**, just off the A22. We join the route at the car park at Wp.12. At **The Eight Bells** pub, **Jevington** Wp15, we turn left along the village street, re-joining the route at **The Hungry Monk Restaurant** Wp.10, to return to **Butts Brow**.

From **Folkington Church**, we walk towards the Downs, turning right onto a public byway (Wp.1 0M), the old coaching road linking **Eastbourne** to **Lewes**. We fork left just after some large beech trees up to and through a bridleway gate (Wp.2 13M), away from the coaching road. Following the path and passing a marker post, we

Access by car:
From **Polegate** take the A27 from the junction with the A22, in 0.6 miles turn left up **Folkington Road** for 1 mile, park in the vicinity of **Folkington Church**. From the west on the A27, turn right up **Folkington Road** approximately 3 miles after **Drusillas** roundabout.

eventually arrive below the **Long Man** (Wp.3 29M).

Continuing ahead, away from the **Long Man**, we pass through a bridleway gate (Wp.4 36M), turning left up a steep chalky cutting. Ignoring the **South Downs Way** joining from below on our right, we keep to the higher path before heading directly for the summit of **Windover Hill** ahead. On the summit we reach a long barrow (Wp.5 48M), pausing to admire the 360 degree views before heading east along the ridge of the Downs, passing a round barrow before joining the **South Downs Way** at a bridleway gate (Wp.6 52M).

We take the right fork on a wide grass track running round the top of a fantastic valley. As the path levels out, we turn half left, uphill, away from the wire fence (Wp.7 57M). Passing a series of four widely spaced marker posts, we go through a bridleway gate, continue ahead and go through another gate to reach a crossroads (Wp.8 77M).

Turning left, we descend through the woods until, as the path levels out, we come to a marker post (Wp.9 81M). Taking the right fork, we soon cross straight over a bridleway crossroads with a fingerpost.

We descend to pass **Jevington Church**, where we join a tarmac road at a T-junction (Wp.10 94M), opposite **The Hungry Monk Restaurant**. You'd probably expect Banoffee Pie to be an American dish. Well, you'd be wrong! It was first invented here, at the Hungry Monk, in 1972. From Sussex, it's conquered the world!

For Short Walk (A) Turn left along the village street to **The Eight Bells** to rejoin the route at Wp.15.

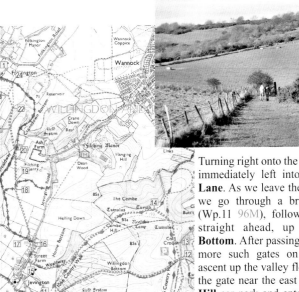

Willingdon Bottom

Turning right onto the road, we turn immediately left into **Willingdon Lane**. As we leave the last cottage, we go through a bridleway gate (Wp.11 96M), following the way straight ahead, up **Willingdon Bottom**. After passing through four more such gates on the gradual ascent up the valley floor, we reach the gate near the east end of **Butts Hill** car park and enter it to find a fingerpost next to a kissing gate

(Wp.12 123M).

(It's from **Butts Hill** car park that **Short Walk (B)** commences.)

Through the kissing gate, we follow the sign for 'Coombe Hill'. We approach the summit of **Cold Crouch**, (with views to the **Eastbourne/Hastings** coastline to our right) then fork slightly left (Wp.13 127M) to pass to the left of the summit following the clearly defined main track round and up towards the next summit. At the top, we pass to the left of a round barrow (Wp.14 135M) on a grass path, continuing along the ridge to cross through a Neolithic camp, its earth embankments just discernible.

Cows cluster at a stile on the descent

Passing to the left of another round barrow, we start descending on a broad, open grass path, crossing three stiles. Just after **Jevington Church** comes into view, we cross a further stile, descending between two wire fences to emerge onto the road opposite the **Eight Bells** pub (Wp.15 160M).

For short walk (B) Turn left along the village street, to rejoin the route at Wp.10 opposite **The Hungry Monk Restaurant**, to return to **Butts Brow** car park.

We cross the road, turning right along the footway, then left at **Green Lane** (Wp.16 163M). After the last house on the right, we turn right at a footpath fingerpost (Wp.17 165M) and cross a stile, turning half left, to go through a steel field gate.

Keeping ahead, diagonally across a field, we cross a double stile and make for and cross another stile at the edge of a wood (Wp.18 174M). We soon join a bridleway and turn right, then as it veers right, we turn left onto a footpath by a fingerpost (Wp.19 175M). Crossing a stile, we follow the path up the edge of a llama field (animals, not spiritual leaders!), then cross a further stile to go through a small wood and join a bridleway (Wp.20 187M).

Here, we go right for 15 yards, then turn left onto a footpath by a marker post. Ascending and descending a series of steps through a lightly wooded area, we emerge to cross a stile into a field. We turn half right towards and past a lone marker post in the middle of the field, continuing to cross a stile (Wp.21 192M), descending on the lower sheep path towards yet another stile below (Wp.22 194M). Over the stile, we follow the path across the field to join a farm track (Wp.23 198M). Turning right, we head downhill to join the old coaching road (Wp.24 200M) where we turn left to return to **Folkington Church** (Wp.1 204M).

5 LULLINGTON HEATH NATIONAL NATURE RESERVE

The rewards of this walk are, at times, breathtaking; everything you could want is here - a real gem. We start from the picture book village of **Alfriston**. Our route takes us across fields to **Wilmington**, passing the remains of a Benedictine priory, and the **Long Man**. We climb **Windover Hill** to start one of the South Downs' longest descents (four miles), through this stunning nature reserve and down to **Charleston Manor**. We return via the pretty flint village of **Litlington** and up the west bank of the **River Cuckmere**, passing **The Old Clergy House** and the 'Cathedral of the Downs', back to **Alfriston**, spoilt for choice with tea rooms and inns.

Access by car:
Pay and display parking at the north end of **Alfriston** in **The Willows** car park.

Short Walk
Follow the route to Wp.10, turning right to take the well signposted **South Downs Way** back to the **White Bridge** at Wp.20, for the return through the village (2 hours, 5.2 miles/8.3km).

We leave **The Willows** car park (Wp.1 0M) from its south end, crossing the road to head into the village along the footway. Just after the **Market Cross**, now more stump than cross, we turn left down **River Lane**. On reaching the raised footpath on the riverbank, we turn right to the **White Bridge** and cross the tidal **River Cuckmere**, then turn left through a kissing gate (Wp.2 6M) to walk up the opposite bank. Passing through kissing gates either side of a road, we follow a diagonal path across two fields and through two kissing gates to emerge onto a road (Wp.3 17M) where we turn left until, just as we pass the shocking pink **Milton Court**, we come to a fingerpost on the right, signed 'Milton Street'.

Across the stile, we turn left and immediately right to the remains of a nearby stile, heading left again across a large arable field. At its far side we cross a stile either side of a narrow road (Wp.4 26M). Following the footpath diagonally across a small meadow, we cross another stile, keeping ahead to go through a footpath gate with a choice of three directions (Wp.5 28M). To visit **The Sussex Ox** pub, turn right.

Our route continues straight ahead, crossing a field to go over stiles either side of a sunken road. Soon crossing another stile, we head across a large field towards our distant destination of **Wilmington Church**, once part of a 13th century Benedictine Priory. On reaching a wide gap in a hedge, we follow the path ahead which soon doglegs right towards the church, and after crossing a narrow road, a gate takes us into the churchyard (Wp.6 42M). We pass an ancient yew tree, reputed to be a thousand years old, held up by a 'Heath Robinson' arrangement of poles and chains, and descend to a road.

Leaving the church, we keep right along a raised footway with glimpses of the priory ruins to our right. We pass the flint-walled village pound, once used for securing stray animals. Opposite the entrance to a car park, we go up steps (Wp.7 46M), following a raised footpath signed 'Footpath to Long Man'.

Near the Long Man

Passing through a squeeze we turn left away from the road, heading towards the **Long Man**, then go through a bridleway gate and ahead to its very base by a wire fence, where we turn left (Wp.8 58M). Following the terraced bridleway, we reach a marker post (Wp.9 66M), doubling back to the right to climb a steep, wide, grassy path.

At the top, we turn to admire the **Weald** laid out below us before going through a bridleway gate, keeping ahead to a wire fence where we join the **South Downs Way** (**SDW**) (Wp.10 78M).

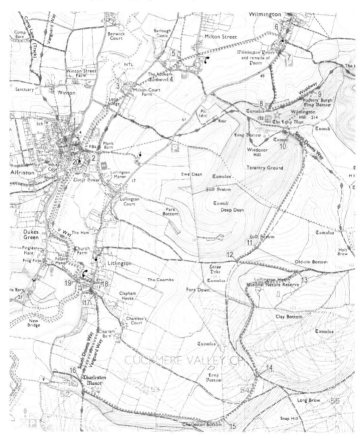

For the short walk
Turn right to follow the well signposted 'South Downs Way' back to the **White Bridge**, re-joining the route at Wp.20.

For the main route

We turn left, skirting round the rim of a spectacularly beautiful deep valley on the wide grass track to start the long but stunning descent to **Charleston Manor**. We soon leave the **SDW**, walking parallel with the fence line round to the right, eventually passing through a bridleway gate and continuing ahead. A bridleway gate (Wp.11 99M) takes us into **Lullington Heath National Nature Reserve**, the finest remaining example of chalk heath in Britain.

Lullington Heath National Nature Reserve

Chalk heath occurs where acid soils have been deposited on chalk, allowing both acid and alkaline loving plants to grow. The reserve is alive with songbirds galore in the spring, including nightingales. Fifty species of birds have nested here, and thirty-four varieties of butterflies have been spotted. In August, parts of the reserve are pink with the flowers of bell heather. Grazing is left to Exmoor and New Forest ponies, Welsh Beulah and Scottish Hebridian mountain sheep, and a small herd of rare Bagot's goats - scary looking!

We go ahead on a flint track. As the track opens out to a small green, we turn left (Wp.12 103M) to descend on a flint track, but first visiting **Winchester Pond**, slightly hidden on our left. This restored 19th century dew pond is a great place for a picnic lunch stop.

The flint track takes us to the bottom of a valley where we turn right through a bridleway gate by a fingerpost (Wp.13 108M) on a wide, velvety, rabbit-cropped grass path which runs down a beautiful valley bottom. Another bridleway gate takes us out of the reserve and into the lightly wooded **Friston Forest** to continue our descent down the valley floor.

On reaching a six-way junction we bear half right (Wp.14 135M), still continuing down the valley bottom. Passing a marker post, we keep ahead to leave the forest through a bridleway gate (Wp.15 146M). Still sticking to the valley floor and passing through two more gates, we arrive at a marker post where we meet the **SDW** and bear slightly right to skirt the grounds of **Charleston Manor**. After crossing a stile on the right opposite a flint barn (Wp.16 172M) we begin the last significant climb, following the hedge line.

On nearing the top, notice another chalk hill figure across the river valley; the relatively modern **White Horse** of **High and Over** was cut in 1924 to replace its 1838 predecessor.

Across a stile either side of a farm track, we follow the path along the fence line and through a meadow, distant views opening out to **Alfriston** ahead. After passing through a kissing gate, we drop downhill between cottages to emerge through a kissing gate onto a road (Wp.17 186M) where we turn left and immediately right at a T-junction, to walk through the village of **Litlington**.

Passing **The Plough and Harrow** pub, we come to a marker post by a tarmac footpath on our left (Wp.18 189M). A hundred yards further up the road are the famous **Litlington Tea Gardens**. We turn left onto the tarmac path, turning left at the riverbank to cross the water on a wooden footbridge (Wp.19 191M), then turning sharp right to follow the west bank along **Burnt House Brooks** towards **Alfriston**.

Alfriston Church from the river bank

We go through several kissing gates, passing **The Old Clergy House** (the very first property purchased by the National Trust), and the fine **Alfriston Church**, known as the **Cathedral of the Downs**. Back at the **White Bridge** (Wp.20 212M), we turn left away from the river, to a path between two tall flint walls up to the **High Street**.

Turning right, we pass wonderful old buildings and then the **Market Cross**, to retrace our steps back to the car park (Wp.1 217M).

6 ALFRISTON & BISHOPSTONE

A steep climb to the **South Downs Way** before we turn down **Green Way**, an ancient droveway. We descend **Devilsrest Bottom** to visit **Norton** and the delightful **Bishopstone**, climbing back up on a fine terraced footpath, returning by **France Bottom** to walk through **Alfriston** village. Two excellent short walks are the alternatives.

4	3H 40M	10 miles/16.1km	460m / 460m		4

Access by car:
At the **Market Cross, Alfriston**, turn up the narrow **West Street**, passing **The Smuggler's Inn**, and take the second turning on the left, **North Road**, for roadside parking near the school.

Short Walks

(a) 6.3 miles/10.1km (2 hours 20 mins). From **Alfriston** up to the **SDW**, down **Green Way**, returning over the top via **France Bottom**. Follow the route to Wp.4, turning left, taking the left fork, and almost immediately left again down towards Wp.10 for the return.

(b) 3.8 miles/6.1km (1 hour 20 mins). With alternative roadside parking near **Bishopstone Church**, accessed from the A259 between **Seaford** and **Newhaven**. Start from Wp.7, keep left at Wp.4, and in 25 yards turn left across the stile for the return.

We head (Wp.1 0M) up the road (W) towards the **Downs**, the road becoming a track, then a path climbing steeply through woodland, slippery when wet. We emerge, a little short of breath, at a T-junction with a wide chalky track, turning left up to a nearby crossroads by a fingerpost (Wp.2 15M) where we turn right, following the **SDW**.

Near the bottom of Green Way

Passing through a field gate, we keep ahead, following the right fence to go through a bridleway gate. Now we follow the left fence line, with fine views across the **Weald**, to a fingerpost crossroads (Wp.3 34M), where we turn left down the **Green Way**, an old droving road linking **Bishopstone** with **Heathfield**.

We pass through a bridleway gate, with amazing views out to sea, as we descend the track all the way to the bottom. Passing a stunted marker post, we climb the delightful terraced track, traversing up the hillside, emerging between posts at a 4-way junction (Wp.4 60M).

For short walk (a) turn left, directions as above.

We turn right, then in 25 yards turn left over a stile to cross an arable field, panoramic views over **Newhaven** soon appearing (see picture on the next page). Descending to a field corner, we follow the left fence line, then continue between a fence and hedge, emerging over a stile into a hillside

Looking towards Newhaven

meadow. Keeping ahead on the upper track, we gently descend the attractive **Devilsrest Bottom**. At a footpath marker post we turn half right, crossing a nearby stile next to a field gate, then immediately cross a farm track and soon pass through a gate onto a descending flint track. At the hamlet of **Norton** we cross a road to climb a stile (Wp.5 82M), soon bearing left to pass alongside a pond.

After following the left fence/wall line we bear right near an electricity pole up a rising terraced grass path which parallels the main rising track above. Towards the top, we bear left on a faint grass path, along the top of a steep slope, to pass under electricity lines with the village of **Bishopstone** nestling across the valley. Our path leads us through a kissing gate at a wood edge and down a charming, terraced woodland path.

The 8th century doorway

At the bottom we pass through a kissing gate (Wp.6 98M), following the left wall to cross a stile in the corner. Turning half right, we diagonally cross a field towards the church, go over a stile and turn left. In 30 yards we turn right up an anti-slip concrete path before turning left up steps. Crossing the attractive green, we enter the churchyard, turning right to go round the church. The church has a Norman tower but most notable is its Saxon 8th century porch and mass sundial with the name 'Eadric' over the door. Leaving the church through the main gate, we turn right then turning left onto a road.

For short walk (b) park at the roadside near the church.

At the top of a slight rise we turn right between flint buildings (Wp.7 107M) to walk up a wide flint track, keeping right at a fork. As the track bends right, after a hard to spot marker post, we fork left onto a footpath (Wp.8 111M) before crossing a stile to emerge onto a delightful terraced path, high up the valley side, a continuation of the **Green Way**.

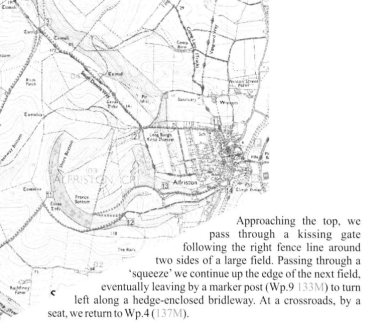

Approaching the top, we pass through a kissing gate following the right fence line around two sides of a large field. Passing through a 'squeeze' we continue up the edge of the next field, eventually leaving by a marker post (Wp.9 133M) to turn left along a hedge-enclosed bridleway. At a crossroads, by a seat, we return to Wp.4 (137M).

For short walk (b) keep left, and soon cross the stile on the left.

Our route takes us hard right, back on ourselves, and in 40 yards we turn left at a T-junction onto a bridleway dropping down the steep, scrub-covered hillside. Reaching the bottom, at a marker post T-junction (Wp.10 146M), we turn left on a bridleway, snaking up and following a right hedge line between arable fields. By a marker post, we change sides to follow the left hedge line steadily up the hill.

At the top, we turn right (Wp.11 162M). Magnificent views soon open out as we follow the left fence down to go through a bridleway gate onto a descending path between fences. Our path veers left, dropping down between fences and then hedges. Immediately after passing adjacent field gates, we turn left over a stile (Wp.12 179M), back on ourselves, onto a fabulous terraced path dropping down to **France Bottom**, sometimes populated with Exmoor ponies which aid scrub control.

At the foot of the slope we turn hard right, following the left fence line along the valley floor, passing through a kissing gate to loosely follow the left fence line down a small meadow. Crossing a stile, we go down another meadow to pass between posts.

By a marker post (Wp.13 198M) we bear left up a steep bank, climbing into light woodland. Our sloping footpath meanders along the hillside, going through a 'squeeze' and over an odd stile with a gate on top. After another squeeze, a stile, and passing between posts, we emerge onto a track, turning right, then immediately left, we make our way down a wide stony track to a T-junction with a road (Wp.14 210M).

The Cathedral of the Downs

Crossing, we turn left along the footway, taking the next right turn, **Tye Road**, towards the **Clergy House** (the first ever property of the National Trust) and lofty church, known as the **Cathedral of the Downs**. Keeping left along the road, we pass cottages to go through a narrow opening in the wall (Wp.15 216M), with a small notice, 'Steps to High Street'.

Going up the steps we cross a courtyard to turn right along the superb **High Street**, with a choice of tea rooms and pubs, passing **The Star Inn**, one of the oldest in England, and **The George** (recommended). At the **Market Cross** we bear left into **West Street**, passing **The Smuggler's Inn**, once the headquarters of the notorious smuggling gang of Stanton Collins. The second turning on the left returns us to **North Road** (Wp.1 221M).

From **Bopeep**, high on the **Downs**, we pass over **Norton Top**, gradually descending on some stunning paths to the **River Cuckmere**. The riverbank path takes us across the **White Bridge** into the lovely village of **Alfriston** for pub or tea-room refreshments, before climbing up to the **South Downs Way** with fine views on the return.

3 | 3H 5M | 7.8 miles/12.6km | 250m / 250m | ↻ | 4

Access by car:
On the A27, at a crossroads within the 40 mph zone, immediately east of **Selmeston**, turn south, up **Bopeep Lane** towards the **Downs**, signed 'By-way'. In 1 ½ miles turn into **Bopeep** car park at the top of the **Downs**.

Short Walk
A high **Downs** walk, returning on **Green Way**, an ancient drove way. Follow the route to Wp.2, turn left, back on yourself, to seek a lovely descending path which then climbs steadily to rejoin the route at Wp.11, turn left along the SDW to return. (1 hour 35 mins, 4miles/6.4km)

Walking back to the car park entrance, we turn left by a fingerpost (Wp.1 0M), heading towards the sea (S) to pass through an adjacent bridleway gate by a field gate, then through another bridleway gate.

Loosely following the left fence line, we go through another gate and keep ahead on a grassy track across a large field with sea views across **Newhaven**. We pass through a bridleway gate by **Five Lord's Burgh** barrow, climbing over **Norton Top** and along the ridge before entering patchy scrub and going through another gate to arrive at a marker post near a seat (Wp.2 35M).

The ridge to the Cuckmere

For the short walk turn hard left, back on yourself, on a descending path.

We take the left fork, along a tree-and-scrub lined track, passing over a crossroads then turning left by a footpath marker post (Wp.3 52M) which appears as the track becomes stone surfaced. The footpath descends a wooded slope, slightly precarious in wet weather, before emerging through a gate onto a scrub and grass hillside which opens out into a beautiful rough organic meadow.

The organic meadow

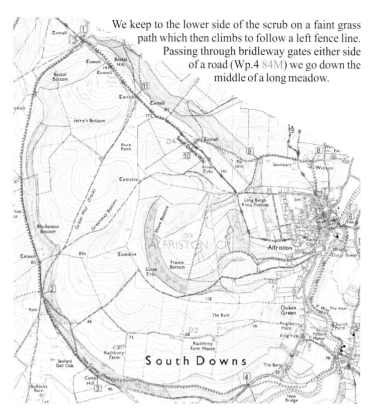

We keep to the lower side of the scrub on a faint grass path which then climbs to follow a left fence line. Passing through bridleway gates either side of a road (Wp.4 84M) we go down the middle of a long meadow.

Passing through a bridleway gate, our indistinct path passes two isolated marker posts, as we look back to the right to spot the **White Horse** cut into the chalk hillside at **High and Over**. We drop down to the **River Cuckmere**, making for and crossing a stile on the raised riverbank. Along the riverbank we pass through a kissing gate to cross the bridge over the river (Wp.5 99M), and turn left up the east riverbank.

The White Bridge

Passing through several kissing gates as we approach **Alfriston** church steeple, we go through another to turn left across the **White Bridge** (Wp.6 123M).

Keeping ahead, we soon pass between tall flint walls to emerge at the **High Street** where we turn right.

After passing **The George** and **The Star** inns, (see picture on the next page) we fork left at the **Market Cross** to pass the inn that can't make up its mind what it's called; either **The Market Inn** or **Ye Olde Smuggler's Inne**.

Once the lair of a famous smuggler, Stanton Collins, the inn has 21 rooms, 48 doors and 6 staircases! We go along **West Street** and soon after passing the junction with **North Road** we turn right onto a footpath (Wp.7 132M).

Emerging over a stile, we cross a meadow and another stile, passing a pretty flint cottage before dropping down to **Winton Street**, where we turn left (Wp.8 138M). We go up the road, keeping ahead at a crossroads onto a farm track to pass through an access land kissing gate (Wp.9 148M) onto a terraced farm track that bears right to traverse the hillside.

Climbing steadily, we benefit from the fine views opening out across the **Weald** and back across **Alfriston** to **Windover Hill**. At the top we bear left between fences, passing through a bridleway gate to turn right at a T-junction (Wp.10 163M) onto the **SDW**. Following the right fence line we pass through a bridleway gate, then follow the left fence line over the first summit to a crossroads fingerpost (Wp.11 175M). We keep ahead, passing a dry dew pond and barrows, as we go over the next summit, dropping down to return to the car park (Wp.1 186M).

A simple, high downland walk, with spectacular views en route, at its best on a clear day.

* No refreshments en-route but there's **The Ram Inn**, in the nearby village of **Firle**.

Access by car: From the A27 east of **Lewes**, take the turning signed 'Firle'. Follow the road straight ahead for 1¼ miles up to **Firle Bostal**, to the car park at the top of the Downs.

Short Walk
Follow the route description to the lowest point (Wp.6), and turn left up **Stump Bottom**, following the bridleway past **Blackcap Farm** to the car park. (1 hour 50 mins, 4.7 miles/7.6km)

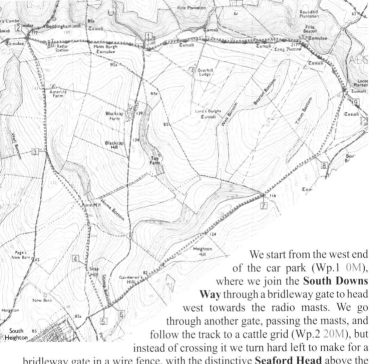

We start from the west end of the car park (Wp.1 0M), where we join the **South Downs Way** through a bridleway gate to head west towards the radio masts. We go through another gate, passing the masts, and follow the track to a cattle grid (Wp.2 20M), but instead of crossing it we turn hard left to make for a bridleway gate in a wire fence, with the distinctive **Seaford Head** above the gate on the horizon.

Going through the gate we follow the track, enjoying views across the **Ouse Valley** and out to sea ahead. As our track becomes flanked by wire fences on both sides (Wp.3 31M) we fork left, up and over **Fore Hill**. Rising to pass a lone bridleway gate, we continue on the track as it veers right over **Snap Hill**.

Bearing left at a marker post (Wp.4 49M), we gradually descend to a T-junction with a wild flower-lined, sunken bridleway (Wp.5 59M), and turn left. At the valley bottom, a bridleway turns left (Wp.6 61M), up **Stump Bottom**.

Descending to the sunken bridleway at Wp.5

For the short walk turn left here, up the valley floor, and past **Blackcap Farm** to eventually return to the car park.

Continuing ahead, we climb steadily up **Gardeners' Hill**, loosely following the right hedge line, and pass through a bridleway gate onto a grass path across sheep pasture. After passing a lone marker post we go through another gate, generally following the right fence line, passing what appears to be a badgers' set on our right, (or extremely big rabbits), and a dry dew pond on our left. Going through a bridleway gate (Wp.7 95M), we continue ahead, noting a large WW2 bomb crater away to the right; hopefully not one of ours!

At a bridleway gate (Wp.8 108M), we fork left, our destination a bridleway gate on the skyline. Going through the gate (Wp.9 120M) we turn left to re-join the **South Downs Way** along the ridge, passing numerous barrows.

Scarp slope near Firle Beacon

When we reach the top of **Firle Beacon** we are rewarded with spectacular views in every direction - **The Weald**, **The Downs** and the **English Channel**. Just past **The Beacon**, on the left, is a rare long barrow, and you may notice that some of the round barrows have a dip in the middle; unfortunately because they were randomly 'looted' by Victorian treasure hunters.

Passing through (or by-passing) two bridleway gates, we head for the car park that's now visible, having overdosed on views (Wp.1 151M). The nearest refreshments are at **The Ram Inn**, in the village of **Firle**.

The 17th century farmhouse of **Charleston**, the home of Bloomsbury artists Vanessa Bell and Duncan Grant, was a gathering place for progressive thinkers and writers of the day, including Virginia Woolf. Their bohemian lifestyle and experimental ideas are reflected in the decorated walls, furniture and garden design of the farmhouse.

During World War II Vanessa and Quentin Bell, with Duncan Grant, decorated the interior walls of **Berwick Church** with both religious and everyday scenes of village life, making the church unique.

Firle village is a delightfully unspoilt estate village, almost a step back in time to an age gone by.

Firle village

3 | 3¼H | 9.4 miles/15.1km | 320m / 320m | 3

Short Walks

(a) (2 hours, 5.2m/8.4km) An outstanding walk, taking in **Firle** village and the Downs of **Firle Beacon**, returning past **Charleston Farmhouse** and **Firle Place**. Follow the route to Wp.5, turning left on the bridleway, descend to cross the coaching road, pass **Tilton Farm**, and turn left at the junction of concrete roads to rejoin the route at Wp.16.

(b) (2 hours 25 mins, 6.9m/11.1km) Alternative roadside parking near **The Rose Cottage** pub in **Alciston**, accessed from the A27. The other half encompasses **Berwick Church**, **Alciston** with its fine tithe barn, an optional detour to **Charleston Farmhouse**, and the Downs above **Alciston**. Walking away from the Downs to pick up the route at Wp.14, turn left on the concrete bridleway at Wp.16 (keep ahead to visit **Charleston Farmhouse** re-tracing steps to continue), pass **Tilton Farm**, cross the old coaching road to climb the Downs and re-join the route at the top by turning left at Wp.5.

Access by car: Take the turning off the A27 east of **Lewes** signed 'Firle' towards the village, turning left in one mile into the village car park immediately after the 30 mph signs.

Returning to the car park entrance (Wp.1 0M), we turn left, passing **The Ram Inn** and bearing right up the village street to pass the excellent **Firle Stores** (village shop and post office). Keeping to the right footway, we keep ahead passing some fine farm buildings onto a stony, then concrete, road, heading towards the Downs. We bear left, following an intermittent flint wall, on a wide stony farm track paralleling the Downs. Immediately before a triangular T-junction, we turn right through a lone bridleway gate (Wp.2 15M), up through a long narrow copse, turning left at a 5-way junction to go through a nearby field gate (Wp.3 20M). We turn right up a field edge before passing through a bridleway gate, keeping ahead on a rising path which traverses left up the scarp slope to connect with the **SDW** joining from our right. After going through a bridleway gate, we pass a round barrow, and soon, on the south side of a fence, a rarer Neolithic long barrow. At the top of **Firle Beacon** (Wp.4 42M) we enjoy a feast of views in all directions. We continue east along the ridge that dominates the landscape, passing round barrows, as we rise to pass a marker post on our left, near the next summit (Wp.5 50M).

For short walk (a) Turn left at Wp.5 down a stunning bridleway, to resume the route by turning left at Wp.16. towards **Charleston Farmhouse**. We continue ahead, dropping down to pass through three gates, as we pass **Bopeep** car park (Wp.6 56M).

The fingerpost at Wp.7

Keeping ahead, we eventually reach a crossroads fingerpost (Wp.7 64M). Turning left on an invisible path, we drop down to cross a stile which soon appears in the fence below, and descend a fine scarp path to cross a stile at the bottom (Wp.8 70M).

We bear right, down the bottom of a sunken footpath, reputedly a smugglers' path used as a route to **Alciston**, hidden from the Excise men. As we reach the old **Lewes/Eastbourne** coaching road, we turn right (Wp.9 76M) towards **Berwick** on the recently stone resurfaced road, previously a nightmare of mud and ruts.

Shortly after passing a fine flint barn, we turn left (Wp.10 90M), still on the wide stony track. Immediately after an aromatic silage bay, we turn right and up, to pass a marker post on a track (Wp.11 93M).

The downs, from the track near Wp.11

Berwick Church

As the track rises and bears left, we turn sharp left by a hidden marker post on a footpath alongside a wall, before turning right up steps, to visit **Berwick Church**.

Leaving the church down a gravel path, we continue between high walls to emerge onto a concrete road where we turn right by the church car park.

At a tiny roundabout, (keep ahead to visit **The Cricketer's Arms**), we turn left, keeping ahead on a concrete road signed 'footpath only'. As the road turns left we continue ahead, dropping down the churned up track to the lower path (Wp.12 103M).

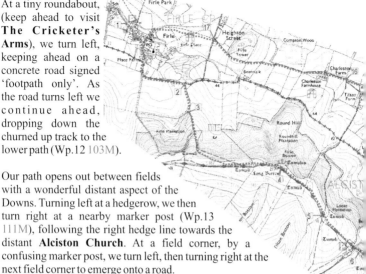

Our path opens out between fields with a wonderful distant aspect of the Downs. Turning left at a hedgerow, we then turn right at a nearby marker post (Wp.13 111M), following the right hedge line towards the distant **Alciston Church**. At a field corner, by a confusing marker post, we turn left, then turning right at the next field corner to emerge onto a road.

The tithe barn at Alciston

Heading right, along the road, we pass the impressive farm and magnificent 14th century tithe barn, once part of a monastery and roofed with 50,000 tiles. We pass close to a medieval dovecote (the nearby church is an optional visit), keeping down through the village, passing **The Rose Cottage** pub, more restaurant than pub, but quite pleasant.

As the road bends left, we turn left by a marker post (Wp.14 128M) up a short track to cross a stile, then follow the right fence line. Crossing stiles either side of a plank bridge, we cross a field diagonally to its opposite corner, where we either cross another plank bridge with stiles, or pass through the gap if it isn't fenced. We follow the right hedge line up to cross a stile onto a road, turning left, and in 35 yards turn right onto a concrete road (Wp.15 140M). Leaving the concrete road by an attractive cottage and pottery, we keep ahead through 4 widely spaced gates, crossing fields before emerging onto a concrete road (Wp.16 155M).

For short walk (b) turn left at Wp.16, following the bridleway past **Tilton Farm**, crossing the old coaching road and climbing to the top of the Downs to turn left, rejoining the route at Wp.5.

Keeping ahead on a concrete road, we pass **Charleston Farmhouse**, a 'must' visit, but check their opening times. We pass through two steel gates onto a somewhat rough farm track, with **Firle Beacon** towering to our left. Through a bridleway gate, we follow the left hedgerow on a grassy track towards the early 19th century **Firle Tower** on the rise ahead, originally used as a gamekeepers' lookout.

Bearing left at a marker post, we go through a nearby bridleway gate then turn right to follow the right hedge line, bearing left at the hedge corner to pass through a gate in the hedge line ahead. We cross two arable fields and an estate track, keeping right, then soon bearing left across another field towards a cottage.

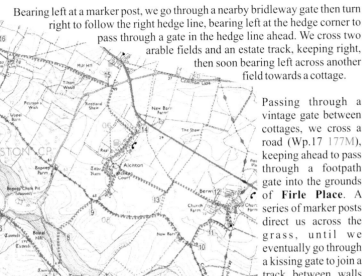

Passing through a vintage gate between cottages, we cross a road (Wp.17 177M), keeping ahead to pass through a footpath gate into the grounds of **Firle Place**. A series of marker posts direct us across the grass, until we eventually go through a kissing gate to join a track between walls into the village.

In the wall to our right, we pass the brick surround to the village spring water supply, the steps worn by time, its clear water still running. Passing some stunning cottages, we turn right by the delightful village stores, returning past the pleasant **Ram Inn** to the start (Wp.1 193M).

10 MOUNT CABURN & SAXON DOWN

To the east of **Lewes** is an isolated outcrop of the South Downs - Neolithic, Bronze and Iron Ages have all left their mark. The attractive village of **Glynde** has a wealth of pretty cottages, the Elizabethan Glynde Place, a unique Georgian church, a working smithy and a charming village stores.

This trailblazing walk includes open access and locally used paths, with some very steep ascents and descents. We start from **The Trevor Arms** pub south of the railway, walking through **Glynde** village, to climb to **Mount Caburn** with amazing views. Turning west we drop down before climbing up for unexpected views across **Lewes** and visit a fascinating memorial. Passing through **Malling Down Nature Reserve**, we climb **Cliffe Hill** and **Saxon Down** before returning down through the village. Recommended for April / May for multitudes of lambs and the profusion of cowslips, particularly on **Caburn**.

4 | 3H 10M | 6.9 miles/11.1km | ↗415m ↘415m | ↻ | ⚠ | 3

Access by car:
From the A27 east of **Lewes**, follow the signs for **Glynde**, with roadside parking near **The Trevor Arms** pub (open all day).

> **Short Walk**
> To visit **Mount Caburn** and the village of **Glynde**, follow the route to **Mount Caburn** then retrace our steps passing Wp.3. keeping ahead to a field gate at Wp.13 and turn right, rejoining our route back to the village (1 hour 20 mins, 3.6 miles/5.8km).

Facing the pub (Wp.1 0M), we turn right to follow the road over the railway bridge and river into **Glynde Village**. We pass the village forge with its horseshoe shaped door, where you can now purchase a longbow and arrows - hopefully you won't need them on this walk. Turning left into **Ranscombe Lane**, we then pass the village stores and soon turn right over a stile (Wp.2 7M) to cross a field. Climbing a stile, we follow the left fence line uphill. Over another stile onto a grass path, we soon cross a track and keep ahead towards the top.

... fantastic views south from Mount Caburn ...

Turning left by a stile (Wp.3 27M), we follow the right fence line. We go over a stile and through a kissing gate as we climb to the summit of **Mount Caburn**, an Iron-Age fort (250 to 50 BC, re-fortified at the end of the Saxon period), with fantastic views over the **Ouse** valley, a tidal estuary when the fort was in use.

From the top we head west, dropping down to cross an access stile in a wire fence (Wp.4 38M), then turning left to follow the fence line along the rim of the deep valley of **Caburn Bottom**, cutting straight across a triangular indentation to maintain direction. At the field corner we turn right then left by a corner with a boundary stone. Our route follows the left fence line steeply down, avoiding the over inquisitive goats and going through a kissing gate at the bottom. We turn right to a nearby stile, then left onto a footpath (Wp.5 56M), down the valley floor.

Passing a dry dewpond, with **The Bible** earthwork on the hill ahead (try as I might I couldn't see the connection), we go through a gate next to a field gate, bearing left to a nearby marker post. We bear right, passing another post, before going through a gate and bearing left to climb the rising terraced path to another gate. Going through, we keep ahead to pass between two posts, continuing on the obvious path to go through a gate in the far corner (Wp.6 80M). We go ahead up a steep bank above the golf course car park, continuing down the left bank alongside a road, with panoramic views across **Lewes** and the riverfront (beware the unfenced section above the cliff).

After dropping down onto Chapel Hill, we turn right before the first house on our left up a short drive (Wp.7 88M), then turn right immediately before a kissing gate to climb steeply up through a light wood, turning left as we emerge at a field. We follow the left hedge to an obelisk (erected in memory of 17 Protestant Martyrs burnt to death outside the Town Hall in **Lewes** in Queen Mary's reign) then turn left at the corner of the field and through a gate (Wp.8 100M), turning right on a woodland path which opens out as we meander down the steep hillside of **Malling Down Nature Reserve** (the odd looking sheep keep the scrub down, although in the recent snow they took a liking to tree bark!).

At a fork we keep left, heading down to a stile on the valley floor below, which we cross (Wp.9 109M), then roughly following the right fence line up a very steep slope to go through a gate near the top (Wp.10 116M). Still following the right fence line, we turn right through a gate by a field gate and in 15 yards turn left through another gate, bearing right on a faint grass path.

Malling Down, descending to Wp.9

We soon follow the fence along the edge of the golf course. As we pass the ninth hole, just beyond the green, we see a relatively rare Neolithic long barrow, cunningly integrated into the course.

With fine views across the Weald and the eastern Downs, we follow the golf course fence until it turns away to the right, by a field gate, we keep ahead turning half left at a boundary stone (Wp.11 136M), onto a wide grass path. Passing through a field gate, we follow the right fence line to a corner near a stile.

We bear right on a grass path to pass the round barrow at the summit of **Saxon Down**. Following the track down over a crossroads, we climb to cross a stile next to a field gate (Wp.12 148M). We pass two fine round barrows as we head south, crossing a stile to follow the right fence line, with the remarkable **Mount Caburn** soon silhouetted against the skyline. As the fence veers right, in 50 yards we turn left by a steel field gate (Wp.13 163M), descending on a grass track to cross a stile. Dropping down a lightly wooded terraced sunken track, we soon keep to the top of the right bank for the best views. Near the bottom we go through a field gate crossing an offset crossroads, ducking under a barrier gate and keeping ahead to turn right down a road (Wp.14 178M).

Glynde church

Descending through the village we pass the entrance to **Glynde Place**, glimpsing the fine griffins through the archway, and pass the Georgian church, an absolute peach, well worth a visit. On the south side of the churchyard is the tomb of farmer John Ellman, the village's most famous man, who worked from 1780 to 1829 to improve the Southdown breed of sheep from a scraggy creature to a worldwide success.

Curiously, he lodged his single workers in his own house until they were married, when he provided them with a cottage, cow, pig, garden and pasture. He also built a school for his workers' children, though would not allow an inn in the village. Hence we return through this stunning village to the Victorian pub, south of the railway, away from the village centre (Wp.1 190M).

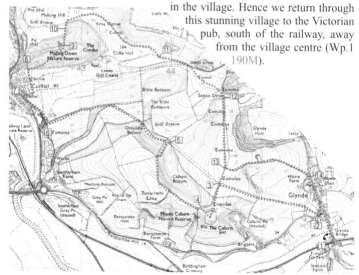

11 THREE STATIONS

A walk linking three stations - starting from **Falmer**, we cross open aspect arable fields to follow a very scenic stretch of the **South Downs Way** then visiting the pretty village of **Southease**, crossing the **River Ouse** before climbing again to the heights and descending to the attractive village of **Glynde**. For most of the walk you can see where we're going and where we've been, as we migrate towards **Glynde**, below the slopes of **Mount Caburn**.

Access by train:
Check train times on:
www.southernrailway.com

Access by car:
From the A27 east of **Lewes**, follow the signs for **Glynde** and park at **Glynde Station**. Catch the train to **Falmer** to start the walk (N.B. poor parking facilities at **Falmer Station**).

Short Walks
(a) Falmer station to **Southease** station, from Wp.1 to Wp.9. (2 hours 55 mins, 8 miles/12.9km)
(b) Southease station to **Glynde** station, from Wp.9 to Wp.13. (1 hour 25 mins, 4 miles/6.4km)

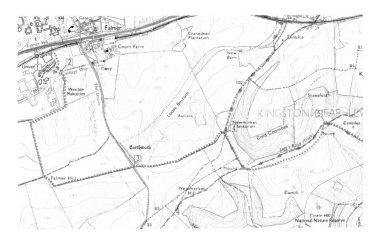

From the westbound platform opposite the booking hall(Wp.1 0M), we go up a brick ramp, through a gate and turn left on a concrete path paralleling the railway. At a concrete road we turn right, turning left at the next junction on a footway passing **Uckfield House**. On reaching a T-junction we cross the road, bearing right to a fingerpost (Wp.2 6M), which points us to a stile.

Over the stile, we turn right up a field edge, going right at a corner and crossing a shallow valley to a field corner marker post where we turn left. After climbing to a marker post crossroads we keep ahead, soon turning left before a marker post to follow the right fence line along a field edge.

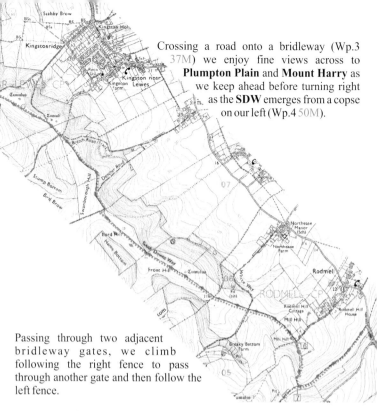

Crossing a road onto a bridleway (Wp.3 37M) we enjoy fine views across to **Plumpton Plain** and **Mount Harry** as we keep ahead before turning right as the **SDW** emerges from a copse on our left (Wp.4 50M).

Passing through two adjacent bridleway gates, we climb following the right fence to pass through another gate and then follow the left fence.

As our path joins with the **Juggs Road** track we keep ahead through a bridleway gate, following the right fence line along the grassy **SDW**. Passing between dew ponds and another bridleway gate (Wp.5 71M) we bear right on the **SDW**; which we'll be following for nearly 7 miles to just before the radio masts at **Beddingham Hill**.

Passing through another bridleway gate our path becomes a flint track with spectacular views across the **Ouse** valley to **Lewes**, **Mount Caburn** and **Firle Beacon**. As tracks drop away to our left, we keep ahead to go through another gate, turning right and then turning left on a gently descending concrete farm track with the distinctive **Seaford Head** in front of us.

Looking across the Ouse Valley to Firle Beacon

As our enjoyable concrete road ends we keep ahead through a gate and along a field edge to pass through gates either side of a concrete road. We dip down before passing through another gate and along a path between fences to emerge on a road at the top of **Mill Hill**.

A pleasant diversion
For a visit to **The Abergavenny Arms** in **Rodmell**, turn left down the road. To re-join our route, follow the directions in Walk 12, from Wp.1 to Wp.4, turning left at **Southease** swingbridge.

We maintain direction through another gate (Wp.6 127M), still on the **SDW** and passing a lone marker post as we drop down to go through another gate before turning left onto a farm track at a T-junction (Wp.7 139M) to go down **Cricketing Bottom**.

Southease swingbridge

Leaving our track as it bears left, we turn right through a gate to follow the obvious path briefly uphill. Going through a gate, we turn left to cross a fairly busy road and guided by **SDW** fingerposts, we turn right along a footway, then left down a road (Wp.8 153M) to stroll through the picture-book village of **Southease**, with its round tower church and pretty village green. Following the road down, we cross the **River Ouse** swingbridge to **Southease** station (Wp.9 166M).

We cross the line carefully through gates either side; beware of the sliding latch that unexpectedly tries to crush your finger! Our road winds through farm buildings to emerge at a busy road where we turn right, crossing the road in 100 yards to go up a bridleway track. We steadily climb through a gate and up a chalk cutting to fork left (Wp.10 183M) and follow the right fence line uphill.

The grassy **SDW** climbs, giving views across the valley and out over the port of **Newhaven**, as we pass through another gate towards the summit, passing a trig point by the dry **Red Lion** dew pond followed by another gate. We go through, or round, a bridleway gate at a fingerpost (Wp.11 227M) to turn hard left down a tatty tarmac road.

Descending the scarp slope, we go through yet another gate to pass farm workers' flint cottages before arriving at the madness that is the A27 (Wp.12 251M). We very carefully cross onto the road to **Glynde**, taking us past **The Trevor Arms** (open all day), before arriving at the station (Wp.13 260M).

A Marbled White feeds on knapweed on the scarp slope

Virginia Woolf, one of the Bloomsbury Set, lived in **Rodmell** at **Monks House** with her husband, Leonard, until her untimely death in 1941 when she filled her pockets with stones and walked into the nearby river.

Starting from **The Abergavenny Arms**, we walk down through the village, passing **Monk's House** before emerging onto the **River Ouse** flood plain. A very pleasant stroll along the riverbank brings us to the hamlet of **Southease**, with its remarkable green and church. We join the **South Downs Way** before turning up to the high Downs, passing **Breaky Bottom Vineyard**, returning on a delightful downland footpath back to **Rodmell**.

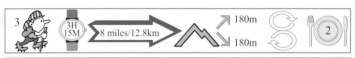

Short Walks
(a) 4.5 miles / 7.2km (1hr 40m). Follow the route description to **Mill Hill** (Wp.9) and turn right down the tarmac road to return to **Rodmell** past the smithy.
(b) 4.5 miles / 7.2km (1hr 40m). From the **Abergavenny Arms** cross the main road and take the tarmac road uphill past the blacksmith's forge to the top of **Mill Hill** (Wp.9) turning right to follow the route description from here.

Access by car:
Rodmell is on the road running from **Newhaven** to **Lewes**, on the west side of the **River Ouse**. Park on the road at the south side of **The Abergavenny Arms** pub.

From the south side of **The Abergavenny Arms** (Wp.1 0M) we head away from the main road (E) down through **Rodmell** village.

The footpath to the church is on our right just before **Monk's House**, once the home of the Woolf family. **Monk's House** is owned by the National Trust and is open on Wednesday and Sunday afternoons, April to October.

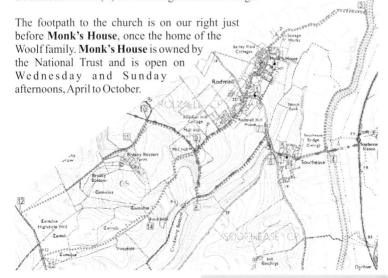

Continuing down, we leave the tarmac road, keeping ahead on an unmade track by the entrance to the **Monk's House** car park (Wp.2. 8M), our track winding its way across the flood plain. Through a bridleway gate, and then a steel gate we continue to a stile on the raised riverbank (Wp.3 26M).

We turn right, crossing the stile, to head downstream along the riverbank. Just before reaching **Southease** swingbridge, we pass a derelict slipway and winch - **Southease** was once a busy fishing village. Going through a bridleway gate, we emerge onto a tarmac road (Wp.4 58M), leading to the swing bridge. We turn right, away from the river on the **SDW**, soon coming to the pretty **Southease** village green and church.

Southease Church, first recorded in 966 AD, is notable for its 12th century wall paintings and its round tower, peculiar to the **Ouse Valley**. In 1604 a widower was remarried at the church; the Parish Register recording the event with a tiny Latin addendum, "A shipwrecked sailor seeks another shipwreck."

Southease Church

Passing the church on our left, we climb the hill towards the main road. Keeping to the right side, we head towards a **SDW** fingerpost (Wp.5 67M), where we turn right along the main road until we soon reach another **SDW** fingerpost. Here, carefully crossing the road, we head up a slight incline to a nearby **SDW** fingerpost (Wp.6 68M), to turn right through a bridleway gate.

We drop down the hill heading for a marker post, where we turn right to follow the path down through a bridleway gate to join a stone track (Wp.7 74M). Turning left we follow the **SDW** up the floor of the **Cricketing Bottom** valley. Before reaching a sprawl of farm buildings, we turn right by a fingerpost (Wp.8 89M). Passing through a bridleway gate we follow the path up a steep hill, to go through another bridleway gate at the top of **Mill Hill** (Wp.9 102M).

Still following the **SDW**, we take the path running down a wooden fence line, to the right of a steel double gate. Emerging through a bridleway gate into the open, we are rewarded with distant views to **Lewes**. After going through a bridleway gate to a crossroads, we leave the **SDW**, turning left onto a twin concrete track (Wp.10 112M). When we reach a fork we turn right, away from the concrete (Wp.11 117M), onto a rough, flinty track, down a steepish hill. In the valley below we can see **Breaky Bottom Vineyard**, first planted in 1974.

At the bottom of the hill our track veers left then right, before starting a gentle climb. We go through a steel footpath gate as the track opens out into a field for us to follow the fence line up the hill to cross a stile.

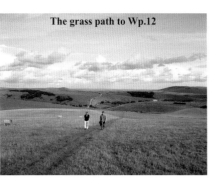

The grass path to Wp.12

A grass path leads us up a wide open field until we reach a footpath gate by a marker post (Wp.12 142M), with sea views across **Saltdean**. Through the gate, we turn left to pass through a steel gate and continue until we reach a footpath gate on our left (Wp.13 152M).

We turn left through the gate, following the path ahead and down to go through another footpath gate. Continuing down an indistinct grass path we pass near a flint-walled sheepfold, a recently restored dew pond, and several round barrows, before eventually making our way to the bottom right hand corner of the field, to go through a footpath gate (Wp.14 174M). We follow the clear grass path down the hill to go through another footpath gate. Our path bears slightly left at the bottom before a steep climb, up an obvious path, brings us back to the top of **Mill Hill** again (Wp.9 191M). We go through the bridleway gate, onto a tarmac road going downhill, eventually passing the village smithy, before returning across the road to **The Abergavenny Arms** (Wp.1 205M).

13 KINGSTON SPECTACULAR

Amazing and beautiful; apt descriptions for this path through a nature reserve, and the descent of probably the finest terraced track on the South Downs, incredibly within a stone's throw of the suburbs of **Brighton**.

From the charming village street of **Kingston**, we climb to the **South Downs Way** to join **Jugg's Road**, used by the fisherwomen of **Brighton** to deliver fish to **Lewes** before the railway era. We enter **Castle Hill National Nature Reserve** using an access land path around an incredibly attractive valley, before descending the wonderful terraced track to **Standean Bottom**. We return up a winding, tranquil valley, for the sharp descent down to **Kingston**, perhaps for refreshment at **The Juggs** pub.

Access by car:	Short Walk
From the A27 roundabout, south west of **Lewes**, take the road signed **K i n g s t o n** turning right in one mile to park in **The Street**, near **The Juggs** pub.	For the delights of the nature reserve and the terraced track, use alternative parking by taking the B123 from **Falmer** on the A27. Turn left into **Bexhill Road** soon after passing the '30mph' signs at **Woodingdean** for roadside parking in the vicinity of N°s 128 to 140. Walk up across the grass to skirt round the end of a wire fence and pass through a bridleway gate 50 yards beyond (Wp.9). Follow the route to Wp.11, keeping ahead up **Falmer Bottom**, through another gate and around field edges to pass through yet another gate, turning right to enter the Nature Reserve. Turn hard left, back on yourself, just before the track becomes enclosed at Wp.8, to rejoin the route (1 hour 40 mins, 4½ miles/7.2km).

Facing the pub, we turn left (Wp.1 0M), up **The Street** towards the Downs, perhaps visiting the plain yet lofty 14th century church with its unusual *tapsel gate*, the central pivot of which offered the advantage of bearing the weight of a coffin whilst awaiting the priest's late arrival! We pass the village pound on our left, once used for securing stray animals, now an allotment! As the road becomes a track we keep ahead through a kissing gate, soon turning left over a stile (Wp.2 11M), following a lightly wooded path to cross another stile.

Curving round the shoulder of the hill

Our path gradually rises into the open to steeply climb left to a stile (Wp.3 16M); across it, we fork right, passing through a minor dip on an unmarked path and curving round the shoulder of a hill to a lone hawthorn tree where we fork left uphill, onto a steep grass path (Wp.4 19M). We climb the grass path to a terraced chalk track, turning left and keeping ahead at the top to a

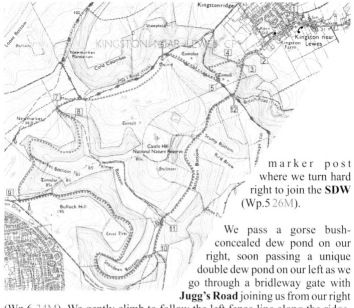

m a r k e r   p o s t where we turn hard right to join the **SDW** (Wp.5 26M).

We pass a gorse bush-concealed dew pond on our right, soon passing a unique double dew pond on our left as we go through a bridleway gate with **Jugg's Road** joining us from our right (Wp.6 34M). We gently climb to follow the left fence line along the ridge, heading west with impressive views.

As we pass through a bridleway gate, the **SDW** soon leaves us. We continue ahead on a stony track to a marker post, leaving **Jugg's Road** as we turn left through a gate into **Castle Hill National Nature Reserve** (Wp.7 51M). We descend a flinty track until, as it opens out, we fork right up an unmarked access land path (Wp.8 54M), climbing up the valley side.

Overlooking Newmarket Bottom

On two occasions as we reach a fork of narrow paths, we keep to the lower, skirting the edge of the gorse and scrub around the shoulder of the hill.

Our path rises up to go round the top of the wonderful valley of **Newmarket Bottom**, complete with dew pond below and swarming with nature.

Going through a small copse, we soon step over a low fence, following the right fence line on a rabbit-cropped grass path (with a remarkable display of yellow gorse in late winter and spring) dropping away to our left.

At the top right corner by a bridleway gate, we turn left (Wp.9 75M), following the right fence line, oblivious to the fact that, a few hundred yards away, the suburbs of **Brighton** begin. We gently descend one of the finest terraced tracks on the South Downs, eventually curving round the badgers' sets at **Standean Bottom**, soon passing through a bridleway gate and down an unexpected row of mature plane trees. At a T-junction at the bottom we turn left on a flint track (Wp.10 106M), passing to the right of abandoned farm buildings, to pass through a bridleway gate (Wp.11 111M).

For the Short Walk, keep ahead to follow the bridleway up **Falmer Bottom** as described above.

Turning right, we pass through a nearby bridleway gate to start our gentle climb up **Balsdean Bottom**, then through three more gates as we gradually wind our way up the valley.

At the top, by a cattle grid, we go through another gate and are soon confronted with a stunning view across the **Ouse Valley** to **Lewes** and beyond.

Expansive views from Wp.12

Keeping ahead we pass a nearby marker post, descending a stony track for 30 yards and turning left down a delightful footpath (Wp.12 137M), towards **Kingston** village below.

Crossing a stile, our path steepens to join our outward route as we cross the stile at Wp.3 (144M). We drop down, keeping left to the lower path before bearing right, retracing our steps over two stiles.

We turn right to pass through the kissing gate and return down **The Street** with its fine selection of old flint cottages and farm buildings. We arrive at **The Juggs** pub (Wp.1 156M), originally two 15th century cottages, only becoming an inn in 1954. It has a pleasing ambience and is deservedly popular (open all day).

From the large village of **Hurstpierpoint**, in the Weald, we head south to climb isolated **Wolstonbury Hill**, an Iron Age hill fort with impressive views. The return, down probably the steepest path on the Downs, takes us past **Danny**, an historic Elizabethan house.

Access by car:
Hurstpierpoint, north of **Brighton**, is on the B2116, accessible from the A273 or the A23. From the mini roundabout by the church in the **High Street**, follow the signs to the main free car park, preferably parking at the west end.

We start from the south-west corner of the car park, exiting between tall walls (Wp.1 0M), to the **High Street** where we turn left. Just past the post office we turn right, then by a fingerpost turn half left, diagonally across a recreation ground. At its far corner we turn right, down a road and in 50 yards, by a letterbox, turn left onto a footpath between fences.

Wolstonbury Hill dominates

As a meadow appears on our right, **Wolstonbury Hill** dominates the view as we keep ahead, soon crossing a stile and turning right at a T-junction to cross another nearby stile. After crossing more stiles either side of two meadows, we enter **Danny Court Park**, ancient Sussex parkland.

Keeping ahead and crossing an estate road, we climb a slope, going over two quite closely spaced stiles before dropping down to a road where we turn right (Wp.2 17M). Shortly after **Bearstakes**, a cottage on our left, we turn left by a fingerpost, crossing stiles either side of two meadows, and turning right at a T-junction of footpaths by a marker post (Wp.3 24M).

We cross another nearby stile, diagonally crossing a meadow, with Jack and Jill windmills on the skyline ahead. Then it's through a kissing gate, following the right fence line to go through a gap in the hedge by a marker post and taking the right fork across a field. We cross two stiles as we turn right into a wood, soon crossing another stile, then turning left along a woodland track. We keep ahead, passing through **Coldharbour Farm** to go up a gravel and tarmac drive, emerging to turn right along a narrow road (Wp.4 37M).

As the road drops down to a dip, we head left up a drive at a fingerpost (Wp.5 40M), passing a ruined barn, and going through a gate to keep ahead up a rough track as we enter National Trust land.

As the track bears right we cross a stile on our left (Wp.6 45M), initially following the right fence line, then crossing an attractive meadow to a stile in the tree line beyond the valley bottom. Crossing into a wood, we go over a track, climbing a flight of steps and eventually emerging over a stile into a meadow. Turning right, we immediately cross a track onto a grassy path, climbing towards the ridge that leads us to **Wolstonbury Hill**. Bearing right onto a track at an angled T-junction, we pass through a bridleway gate, keeping ahead to turn right onto a grass path at a marker post (Wp.7 64M).

'falling' off the edge of the hill

We climb, keeping left at a fork to head for the trig point at the summit, occasionally pausing to reflect on the wonderful views. Maintaining our direction north, we wind through humps and bumps, suddenly feeling we might fall off the edge of the hill but we're soon reassured, as the path down this extremely steep hillside comes into view.

We descend the main path, with **Danny Park** visible below and **Hurstpierpoint** beyond. Dropping straight down through the trees, we cross a stile, keeping right, and in 50 yards turn left at a fingerpost,

down a wide, horse-churned bridleway. After emerging between fences we turn right at a T-junction by a marker post (Wp.8 81M), then turn left at a road junction. As our road bends right by a letterbox, we turn left by a fingerpost, through a small copse, to cross a bridge and stile.

Danny

We keep ahead across a meadow, approaching **Danny**, once the home of the Prime Minister, Lloyd George, with his wife, dog and secretary/mistress. In 1918 his War Cabinet met here to draw up the terms of the World War One Armistice. Crossing a stile, we follow the left fence line to cross another stile onto a 4-way estate road junction (Wp.9 95M).

Taking the road to the right of **Danny**, we follow the right fence line, turning right to cross a stile by a fingerpost. We follow the left hedge line, crossing stiles either side of a plank bridge and forking right by a 3-way fingerpost. We cross a lumpy meadow, a stile and an arable field, to enter a narrow wood. Emerging, we cross stiles either side of a bridge, loosely following a left fence line and bearing left at a 3-way fingerpost (Wp.10 103M).

A nearby stile takes us onto another woodland path, before crossing more stiles and passing down field edges to eventually join a driveway by **Little Washbrook Farm**. As the drive bears left, our route turns right by a marker post (Wp.11 109M), keeping ahead to cross a bridge and stile, a track, a field, and another footbridge and stile.

We climb a fence/wall/hedge enclosed path, to join a track between houses, turning left by a 5-way fingerpost onto a village footpath (Wp.12 114M). Our path becomes a track heading towards the church steeple; we bear right onto a road, by the 'Parish Rooms', back to the **High Street**, where we turn left, then first right, to return to the car park (Wp.1 119M).

15 BATTLE OF LEWES

English history was created on this turf, on the site of a battle that shaped the principle of parliamentary representation. Early one morning in 1264 on the Downs to the west of **Lewes**, Simon de Montfort and the Barons' army climbed the steep scarp slope unobserved, towards Mount Harry. Turning east along the ridge, they formed up to launch a feint attack towards the castle with the main thrust intended towards the **St. Pancras Priory** where King Henry III was based. The King's army, taken by surprise, quickly formed up on the lower ground. Prince Edward attacked the Barons' left flank, routing the Londoners division, chasing them down the north slopes of the **Offham Quarries**. The Prince was then lured into the **Weald** to attack de Montfort's banner, deliberately left in the rear for this purpose. With Prince Edward out of the picture, the Barons attacked, forcing the King's troops down the hill, to the south-east of the racecourse, and back towards the **Priory**, where the King ultimately surrendered and the Mise of Lewes was signed.

From **Plumpton**, we walk away from the Downs before turning towards **Mount Harry**, following Simon de Montfort's route up the scarp slope. We pass the old **Lewes** racecourse near the site of the main battle, and drop down through the amazing **Offham Quarries**, turning west to climb back to **Blackcap** and down a delightful woodland track to **The Half Moon** pub at **Plumpton**.

Access by car:
The Half Moon pub at **Plumpton** is on the B2116 which runs from **Ditchling** to **Offham**, near **Lewes**. Turn up **Plumpton Lane** at the pub, parking in a lay-by on the left, approximately 75 yards from the junction.

Short Walks
(a) From **The Half Moon** to Wp.8, then turn right towards **Blackcap** (Wp.19) to return. (3.6 miles / 5.8km, 1¼ hours)

(b) Alternative parking in the lane opposite **The Blacksmith's Arms** at **Offham** on the A275. Start the walk from Wp.15, turning sharp left at Wp.8. for the return leg. (4.2 miles / 6.8km, 1½ hours)

We head north from the lay-by near **The Half Moon** (Wp. 0M), away from the Downs, crossing the road to a footpath fingerpost and going over a stile to cross a small field. Going through a footpath gate next to a high flint wall, and attracting the inquisitive stares of the llamas, we follow the wall and fence to go over a stile (Wp.2 3M), then turn half left on a diagonal path across an arable field, heading towards the south end of a wood.

On reaching the wood we turn half right along its south edge to a marker post by the corner of a field, where we turn left (Wp.3 8M) and across a tarmac driveway to a fingerpost. Here we turn half right, diagonally across an arable field, towards a stile in the distant hedge. Crossing stiles either side of a tarmac road (Wp.4 14M), we follow the hedge line towards a group of farm buildings.

On reaching a road we head left, soon passing a cottage where we turn right by a fingerpost onto a twin concrete track. Passing through the north end of **Warningore Farm** yard to a marker post, we turn right onto a bridleway (Wp.5 20M) which leads towards **Mount Harry**, following in the footsteps of Simon de Montfort's troops in 1264.

We pass through three bridleway gates as we head to the Downs to reach and cross a road (Wp.6 30M) and follow the bridleway as we start our ascent. After going through a wooden gate, we eventually go over a crossroads by a marker post (Wp.7 36M) onto a fairly steep, winding path towards the top of the Downs, emerging from the scrub and keeping ahead to pass a fingerpost (Wp.8 44M).

For Short Walk (a)
Turn right here, heading for Wp.19 at the top of **Blackcap** to follow the route back.

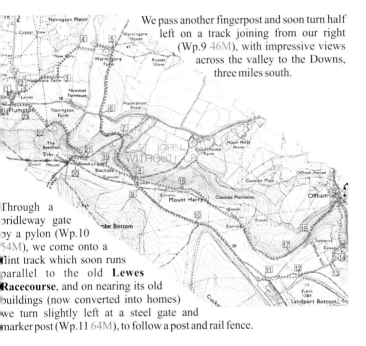

We pass another fingerpost and soon turn half left on a track joining from our right (Wp.9 46M), with impressive views across the valley to the Downs, three miles south.

Through a bridleway gate by a pylon (Wp.10 54M), we come onto a flint track which soon runs parallel to the old **Lewes Racecourse**, and on nearing its old buildings (now converted into homes) we turn slightly left at a steel gate and marker post (Wp.11 64M), to follow a post and rail fence.

Through a bridleway gate, we follow the grass path to the right side of the hedge line ahead. In the fields away to our right is the site of the Battle of Lewes of 1264, with the Barons' army formed up on our left and Henry's army on the lower slopes to our right. Passing through a bridleway gate, we keep left to pass through another nearby gate (Wp.12 69M), following the fence line, which later turns half left up a slight incline and through a bridleway gate (Wp.13 73M).

After 20 yards we turn left and over some scaffold, to walk round the rim of a disused chalk pit, with spectacular views across the **River Ouse** flood plain to **Saxon Down** and **Mount Caburn**. Beware of the cliff edge protected by a ramshackle wire fence!

... spectacular views across the Ouse valley ...

We take the right fork by a marker post downhill (Wp.14 76M) through a lightly wooded area, following Prince Edward's route as he pursued the hapless Londoners into the **Weald** below.

As we descend we keep to the right, through the old quarry workings, taking care as the path can be slippery. Stepping over a scaffold, we continue down to a marker post near a road (Wp.15 85M).

For refreshments at **The Blacksmith's Arms**, continue to the road and turn left for 100 yards.

For Short Walk (b)
We park down the lane opposite the pub, walk back to the main road, and turn left then right to go ahead at Wp.15.

At Wp.15 we turn left to start the climb back to the top of the Downs. After going through a bridleway gate on the right (Wp.16 93M), we turn left up a stunningly beautiful woodland path. Passing through a bridleway gate, we keep ahead until the path bears left just before a fallen tree and we emerge at a field by a marker post (Wp.17 97M) where we turn right along the top edge of a wood, passing a marker post and keeping ahead on a grass path to go through a bridleway gate.

We follow a wide rabbit-cropped grass path, cross a field, pass under power lines and thread our way through some gorse bushes to a bridleway gate. Following the track to the right of a clump of trees, we arrive at the summit of **Mount Harry** (Wp.18 116M). We continue ahead, revisiting our old friend, the marker post (Wp.8 122M).

Looking towards Blackcap from Mount Harry

For Short Walk (b)
From **The Blacksmith's Arms**, turn sharp left towards Wp.9 to follow the route back.

We head for the top of **Blackcap** (Wp.19 126M), crowned with trees planted at the time of the 1953 Coronation. Still heading west along the ridge, we descend until, 50 yards before reaching a bridleway gate next to a field gate, we fork right (Wp.20 131M).

Passing a number of round barrows on our right, we come to a marker post and follow the flint track to the right down a cutting. At a gap, we climb to the top of the left hand bank to enjoy superb views. We drop down to a marker post (Wp.21 134M) where we turn sharp left, this time opting to scramble down the top of the right hand bank for the best viewpoint.

Dropping down to Wp.21

A steel gate takes us onto a beautiful beech-lined and terraced woodland descent. We keep left on the main path at a footpath marker post, and at another marker post towards the bottom (Wp.22 143M), turn left onto a footpath, dropping down to cross a nearby stile at the edge of a field. We follow the path across the field, cross a stile and continue ahead to the far corner of the next field. Just before the road, we cross a stile (Wp.23 148M) and turn left onto the footpath paralleling the road.

As the path drops down to the road we walk along the left footway, then cross the road at **Plumpton Lane** (Wp.24 150M) to return to our start point, or visit the pub. **The Half Moon** has a large, child friendly garden, and on our visit served extraordinarily large portions of food!

The Downs above **Plumpton** were once populated with thriving farming communities. We pass through the site of a late Bronze Age settlement on **Plumpton Plain** and view some of the finest Romano-British field systems and lynchets on the Downs at **Buckland Bank**.

From **The Half Moon** at **Plumpton** we ascend on a stunning wooded path up the scarp slope, to gently drop down through the rich woodland of **Ashcombe Bottom**. We cross the open Downland around **Buckland Bank**, returning across a pretty valley to steadily climb back before descending a fine path with impressive views across the Weald.

3 | 2H 40M | 6.3 miles/10.1km | 325m 325m | ↻ | 3

Access by car:
The Half Moon pub at **Plumpton** is on the B2116, which runs from **Ditchling** to **Offham**, near **Lewes**. Turn up **Plumpton Lane** at the pub, parking in a lay-by on the left, approximately 75 yards from the junction.

Short Walk
Follow the route to Wp.4 turning right along the South Downs Way. Take the next bridleway on the right to rejoin the route at the top of the scarp slope at Wp.10 (1hour 20 mins, 3.5 miles / 5.6km).

From the lay-by near **The Half Moon** (Wp.1 0M), we walk back towards the T-junction, crossing the road and turning left (E) along the footway, soon becoming an elevated footpath. At a stile we turn right (Wp.2 4M) on a diagonal footpath across an arable field. Crossing two stiles, we enter a wood, turning right in 20 yards at a T-junction. We climb steadily up the wooded scarp slope track, with tantalising glimpses eastwards through the trees. Going through a steel gate, we clamber onto the top of the left bank for superb views as we climb to a T-junction (Wp.3

... tantalising glimpses ...

... superb views from the top of the left bank ...

19M), turning right up a sunken flint track. At the top, after crossing the **South Downs Way (SDW)** (Wp.4 22M) and passing a National Trust 'Blackcap'sign, we turn slightly left down a meadow, going through a bridleway gate which appears in a fence along the wood edge.

We enter **Ashcombe Bottom**, a mix of mature woodland, glades, coppicing and scrub, a haven for wildlife including glow-worms, dormice, over fifty species of birds, and butterflies such as the white admiral and silver washed fritillary.

We follow the meandering track, which can be muddy in wet weather, all the way down the shallow valley bottom, accompanied by the sound of croaking pheasants, the laughing cackle of the green woodpecker and songbirds various.

Towards the bottom, at a fork by a marker post, we take the unofficial route to avoid a horse churned track by keeping right and passing through a field gate. We cross the field to pass through a bridleway gate, turning right to rejoin the bridleway. We go through another gate turning right to go through yet another gate (Wp.5 53M), then turn half left on a grass path to enter a small wood at the top of the hill.

Emerging into open Downland, we pass a marker post to continue uphill in noisy skylark country. Passing through a bridleway gate next to a double field gate, almost immediately turning left through another gate (Wp.6 66M). We turn half right passing through yet another nearby gate and turn half right following the faint grass path around some stunted trees to pass above two *lynchets* (Iron Age banks caused by the very gradual migration of ploughsoil down the slope to the bottom edge of the small fields). Looking down the valley, the field patterns, banks and hedge lines of the Romano-British period are clearly visible.

As a fence appears, we keep to the right side, going uphill to pass through a bridleway gate (Wp.7 78M), turning to look back to the ancient landscape before crossing a flint track and arable field to a nearby marker post at a T-junction.

The view back from Wp.7

Turning left, we follow the right fence line above **Moustone** valley, eventually turning back on ourselves through a gate at a marker post (Wp.8 94M).

The attractive terraced path

We descend an attractive terraced path, passing through a bridleway gate on our way to the valley bottom. Climbing up the opposite side, we follow the right fence line up the long dip slope, passing through three bridleway gates and going through a scattered clump of stunted trees, the site of a late Bronze-Age village.

Eventually we reach the top, through a gate, to cross the chalk track of the **SDW** (Wp.9 129M). Going ahead through an access land kissing gate, then passing a round barrow, we make our own path, turning right along the top of the scarp slope, keeping above the tree line and enjoying the views across the Weald. Reaching a marker post (Wp.10 137M), we turn hard left, dropping down a narrow terraced path clinging to the steep slope. We go through a gate, turning right onto a concrete track, turning left through a steel gate in fifty yards (Wp.11 144M) onto an attractive descending track. Keeping to the top of the right bank, we follow the path to eventually rejoin the track, then pass through two steel gates to emerge at a road (Wp.12 154M).

Crossing, we follow the access road to **Plumpton College**, turning right in seventy-five yards through a footpath gate on a well tended grass path between fences, with the Elizabethan **Plumpton Place** below on our left. Crossing a stile, we make for the far right corner of a meadow. Going over a stile and passing in front of **The Half Moon**, we turn left into **Plumpton Lane** to return to the start (Wp.1 160M). The pub has a large, child friendly garden, and on our visit served generous portions of food!

17 STANMER PARK AND DITCHLING BEACON

Stanmer Park, 18th century house, unspoilt village and church, is owned by the City of Brighton and Hove and has been protected from development. There is also a fascinating rural museum open on weekend afternoons (Easter to October).

Stanmer Church

From **Stanmer House** (c.1724) we walk up through some magnificent cypress trees into **Great Wood**, gradually climbing all the way up to the fabulous viewing point of **Ditchling Beacon**, one of the highest points on the **South Downs**. We enjoy impressive views in all directions as we go east along the **SDW** before we turn down some delightful paths to reach unspoilt **Stanmer Village** with its tearoom, farm buildings, well house and Church.

Short Walks

(a) (1hour 25 mins, 3.8 miles/6.1km) Follow the route description to **Highpark Corner** (Wp.7). Turn right on the well used public footpath, passing **Highpark Farm**, to re-join the main route turning right by the pylon at Wp.16.

(b) (1 hour 45 mins, 4.8 miles/7.7km) Alternative car parking at **Ditchling Beacon** car park. Follow the route description from Wp.10. At Wp.16 turn right onto the public footpath, passing **Highpark Farm**, to re-join the route at **Highpark Corner** (Wp.7) crossing the road for the return to **Ditchling Beacon**.

Access by car:

The entrance to **Stanmer Park** is accessed from the **A270 Brighton** to **Lewes** road, northbound only. On entering the park continue ahead for ¾ of a mile and park in the vicinity of **Stanmer House**.

Facing the front door of **Stanmer House** (Wp.1 0M), we turn left then right, into the 'back garden' of the house. Passing up the lawned slope, through some huge cypress trees, we enter **Great Wood**, almost immediately joining a crossing path (Wp.2 6M), where we turn right. This path goes slightly downhill before bearing left and continues to a huge log. We bear left, then immediately right to take the left fork (Wp.3 11M), which goes steadily uphill. The woods were very badly damaged by the hurricane of 1987; uprooted trees and rotting logs showing its extent.

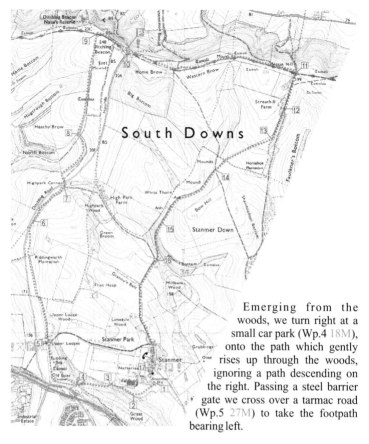

Emerging from the woods, we turn right at a small car park (Wp.4 18M), onto the path which gently rises up through the woods, ignoring a path descending on the right. Passing a steel barrier gate we cross over a tarmac road (Wp.5 27M) to take the footpath bearing left.

Leaving the woods we cross a stile and then another, turning half right up the edge of the field. Just after a dew pond we cross another stile (Wp.6 47M) and bear half right into a small wood. When we reach a marker post on the right, 'Highpark Corner', we turn left (Wp.7 54M).

For the shorter walk from Stanmer
Turn right at Wp.7, following the well used public footpath, to rejoin the route by turning right at the pylon at Wp.16.

Making our way towards the nearby road, we cross to a bridleway fingerpost and follow the path downhill in the direction indicated. Going through a steel bridleway gate we turn sharp right to walk around the top edge of a field. Arriving at a steel field gate (Wp.8 65M), we head uphill on a wire-fenced track to pass through a steel cattle pen and continue ahead to go through a bridleway gate. Maintaining direction we pass through a bridleway gate (Wp.9 81M), and are suddenly confronted by the stunning view across the **Weald** with **Ditchling** village below.

We turn right onto the **SDW**, passing **Ditchling Beacon** (the highest point of the eastern Downs). We go through a bridleway gate and soon reach a road (Wp.10 91M). This is the starting point for the shorter walk, parking in the adjacent car park, where, incidentally, there is usually an ice cream van. Crossing the road we go through a bridleway gate, next to the highest dew pond on the Downs, to continue along the **SDW** ignoring all turnings off while enjoying the panoramic views. We drop down to go through a bridleway gate, cross a tarmac road and in 20 yards we turn right through a bridleway gate (Wp.11 134M).

Walking down the edge of the field, we pass **Street Hill Farm**, and reach a bridleway gate (Wp.12 139M). Through the gate we turn half right to cross a stile 15 yards away and turn left. We cross a stile by a small barn, continuing ahead down the left edge of a field. When we reach a footpath marker post on our left (Wp.13 144M), we turn half right on a clearly defined grass footpath. Crossing a stile, we drop down to a crossroads, going ahead through a bridleway gate (Wp.14 154M).

We gently descend a grass path down a beautiful valley to go through a bridleway gate. With woods on our right, we continue down **Moons Bottom** to yet another bridleway gate (Wp.15 169M). We go through the gate to steadily ascend a wide woodland track leading to a crossroads by a pylon (Wp.16 177M).

Descending below Wp.14

For the shorter walk from Ditchling Beacon
Turn right at Wp.16 on the footpath which passes **High Park Farm**, to re-join the route in ¾ of a mile at Wp.7 where we turn right crossing the nearby road to return.

We go straight ahead at Wp.16 on a flinty track, which rises slightly before descending towards **Stanmer Village**. After passing several barns, we pass through a bridleway gate by a pond, to walk down through the attractive village. We pass **Stanmer Tea Rooms** and various interesting farm buildings, before reaching a T-junction (Wp.17 194M) with a small flint building ahead to the left. This building is the village well house, powered by a donkey wheel - one of only three in Sussex. A 36 gallon bucket could be drawn from the 250ft shaft. Having hauled the water up, the donkey had to be turned round in the wheel to lower the bucket down again – since even the most intelligent of donkeys failed to master the art of walking backwards!

We turn right, to pass the church, where we turn left, back to **Stanmer House** (Wp.1 197M).

Jill

During the Great War, injured Indian troops were treated at Brighton's Royal Pavilion, used as a hospital. The Hindus and Sikhs who died were cremated at this moving place, granite slabs now covering the cremation sites before the shining white marble temple. On the brighter side we visit a pair of windmills; **Jill**, the white post mill was built in 1821 and dragged all the way from Brighton by a huge team of oxen in 1852, and **Jack**, the brick tower mill (1866), now a private residence. From the car park alongside **Jill** we head east above the scarp slope overlooking the **Weald** and turning south by **Ditchling Beacon** to gently descend a tranquil valley before our visit to the **Chattri**. A gentle scenic climb returns us to the arms of **Jill**.

| 3 | 2H 25M | 6.9 miles/11km | ⛰ | ↗ 230m ↘ 230m | ↻ | 🍴 0 |

Access by car: Take the A273 from the A23 at **Pyecoombe**, signed 'Hassocks', turning right just over the brow of a hill by a brown 'Windmills' sign, up the narrow lane to park alongside **Jill**.

Short Walk

To visit the **Chattri**, follow the route to Wp.3, turn right to follow a footpath south to a marker post by Wp.7 at the junction with a well-used farm track, then turn right to re-join the route (1 hour 40 mins, 4.8 miles/ 7.7km).

Starting from the north-west end of the car park (Wp.1 0M), we pass through a kissing gate, turning right to go through a nearby gate onto a path between fences. At a T-junction we turn left on a stony track, forking left at a fingerpost onto the **SDW** (Wp.2 5M). Passing through a gate we continue, eventually going through a bridleway gate at the top of the slope in the left fence (Wp.3 19M) where we turn right, passing a substantial fingerpost amusingly pointing to 'Eastbourne and Winchester'.

On top of the scarp slope

We follow a faint access land path, initially following the right fence line before gradually bearing left to join a visible sheep track running along the top of the scarp slope with inspiring views across the **Weald**. After crossing a stile, we're soon following the right fence line, safe in the knowledge that we won't be run down from behind by a silent cyclist from the nearby **SDW**!

Passing through a kissing gate, our path rises slightly before running along the top of the scarp slope to a distant marker post, visible on the skyline, where we bear right to a bridleway gate (Wp.4 38M) by an ex-dew pond surrounded by a

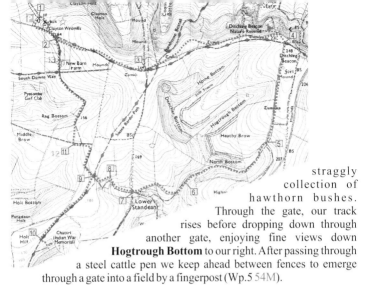

straggly collection of hawthorn bushes. Through the gate, our track rises before dropping down through another gate, enjoying fine views down **Hogtrough Bottom** to our right. After passing through a steel cattle pen we keep ahead between fences to emerge through a gate into a field by a fingerpost (Wp.5 54M).

Keeping ahead on a faint grass bridleway down to the delightful valley bottom, we then pass through a gate. We gently descend down a long narrow meadow, eventually passing through a bridleway gate in the right fence line, then follow the left fence line along the valley floor. By a marker post (Wp.6 70M), we fork right onto a flinty track, gradually rising up the hillside ahead.

Passing through a bridleway gate, we drop down to go through another gate, turning right at a T-junction, passing some rather squalid cattle pens to a nearby marker post (Wp.7 82M). We climb uphill on a well-used farm track, keeping to the right of a marker post and following the left fence line to pass through the gate at the top (Wp.8 87M); turning left, we follow the left fence line around a field, turning left at the top of the slope by a crossroads marker post (Wp.9 90M).

We pass, or go through, an isolated copse, eventually turning left through a bridleway gate (Wp.10 103M) and descending to pass through another nearby bridleway gate to enter the **Chattri** grounds. We retrace our steps, passing the copse and turning left at the crossroads marker post (Wp.9 115M), to follow the left fence line.

The Chattri

After going through a bridleway gate we turn right between fences, then go through another gate, turning left and going downhill to a marker post (Wp.11 121M) to then turn right on a rising track, soon dropping down alongside the golf course at **Rag Bottom**. Should there be any golfers on the tees, wait until they have teed off, just in case! We keep ahead at a crossroads on a track between fences, passing **New Barn Farm** and keeping left at the junction to gently descend back to **Jill** (Wp.1 145M). **Jill** is a post mill (open Sunday afternoons, April - September), the whole contraption, quite amazingly, pivots on a post, moving according to the wind direction.

Perhaps the best known beauty spot on the South Downs, **Devil's Dyke** has attracted visitors since Victorian times, when it boasted a railway line from **Hove**, a cable car across the **Dyke**, a mountain lift from **The Weald**, and all the trappings of the fairground (sounds like a Victorian version of Land's End). On Whit Monday of 1893, no less than 30,000 people visited the **Dyke**! Fortunately, it's back to being a beautiful place, with only a modern pub remaining.

It's a figure of eight walk, which splits into two fine short walks. Starting from the very attractive **The Shepherd and Dog pub** at **Fulking**, we climb to classic views from the high Downs and drop down the deep valley that is the **Devil's Dyke**. Passing near **The Royal Oak** at **Poynings** we follow a chalk stream into **The Weald**, passing through the village of **Fulking**, ascending again to visit one of the secret places of the South Downs, **Castle Rings**, before descending on a stunning footpath to return across **The Weald**. Apologies for the 29 stiles we have to climb!

Access by car:

From the A2037 between **Upper Beeding** and **Small Dole** follow the sign for **Fulking**, or from the A281 follow the sign to **Fulking**. Park in the lay-by next to a stream near **The Shepherd and Dog**.

Short Walks

(a) Fulking and **Devil's Dyke**. Follow the route to Wp.11, turning right to return to **The Shepherd and Dog** pub (1 hour 50 mins, 4.2 miles/6.9km).

(b) Fulking and **Castle Rings**. Walk up the road from **The Shepherd and Dog** to pick up the route at Wp.11, passing through the village (1 hour 35 mins, 3.8 miles/6km)

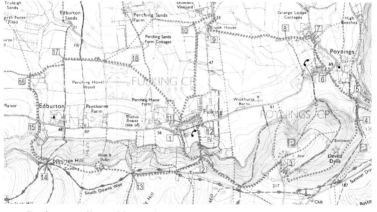

By the eternally gushing spring water, we enter **The Shepherd and Dog** car park (Wp.1 0M), keeping left to a rising footpath between hedges, soon following a left fence line up towards the South Downs. Crossing a stile, we climb steps onto a wide terraced grass path that climbs steeply, to go over a deeply cut crossroads (Wp.2 9M). Our steep path curves right onto another terraced path traversing up the scarp slope. We go through a bridleway gate, keeping ahead to a marker post and crossing over a sunken crossroads. We gradually curve left, passing through the Iron Age earthworks towards **The Dyke** pub, with wonderful views across **The Weald**.

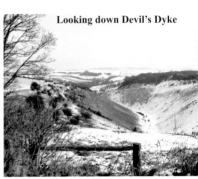
Looking down Devil's Dyke

Going over a stile, we turn right, crossing the road to the right of the pub car park entrance, to a bridleway marked by three posts (Wp.3 30M). Following the path downhill to a nearby marker post, we turn right, dropping down to pass through a bridleway gate, keeping ahead before bearing left to descend the deep cleft that is **Devil's Dyke**. Two hundred years ago, the Great Bustard was hunted with greyhounds here.

At the bottom, we go through a bridleway gate to the right of a field gate (Wp.4 44M), onto a lightly wooded track, descending to cross a stream which we'll encounter several times along our way. At a fork we keep left on a footpath (Wp.5 48M), following the top edge of a gully. We cross a stile into a field, soon crossing another to turn left alongside a duck pond. Climbing a stile, we turn right down a field edge, crossing another stile onto a concrete access leading us to a road (Wp.6 54M). Turning left, we soon cross the road, turning right through a kissing gate (continue up the road to visit the nearby **Royal Oak**), on a footpath leading us through two more kissing gates.

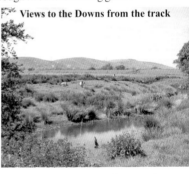
Views to the Downs from the track

In 35 yards we turn left on a footpath, emerging onto the concreted **Mill Lane** (Wp.7 60M) where we turn left, eventually crossing a stile by a gate (Wp.8 64M) onto an attractive track following our stream, which we cross to bear half left to a stile on the skyline ahead. Crossing, we keep ahead following a low ridge across two fields and a stile to eventually cross a stile onto a road (Wp.9 77M).

Turning right, we soon turn left by a fingerpost, immediately after crossing our stream, to go over a stile following a delightful streamside path. We cross a plank bridge and in 35 yards turn left over a footbridge and stile (Wp.10 82M), where we turn half left to follow the right fence line by a fingerpost, then crossing stiles either side of a plank bridge. We follow the right hedge line, crossing three closely spaced stiles, keeping ahead to the right field corner to cross another stile. We immediately turn right through a kissing gate, turning half left at a nearby fingerpost to diagonally cross a field. Climbing steps to go through a kissing gate, we keep left across a small field to go through a gate dropping down to a road (Wp.11 99M). (For short walk (a) turn right, passing **The John Ruskin Memorial Fountain**, to return to the start.)

We turn left through **Fulking village**, passing the village pump, bearing right.

As the road turns left, we turn right onto a track (Wp.12 104M), and in 50 yards turn left up a 'hard to spot' footpath towards the Downs. Crossing a stile, we keep ahead, soon forking right to emerge onto the open scarp slope. We climb steeply straight up to the previously visited sunken crossroads (Wp.2 114M), passing to the right of the marker post, onto the top of the right bank to climb to the top, where we turn right to follow the left fence line along the **SDW**. Crossing under power lines, we go through a bridleway gate (Wp.13 126M) and in 25 yards, turning half right, make for a small clump of trees at the top of the hill. Passing through the wind-bent trees, we cross a stile to enter **Castle Rings**, an 11th century motte and bailey earthwork castle, built by the Normans on the boundary of the Rapes of Lewes and Bramber. There are amazing views, particularly from the north side, a brilliant place for a picnic.

After exploring the **Castle Rings**, we leave over the same stile, turning right towards the extreme right radio mast, before heading downhill to make for a cluster of gates as they come into view.

The terraced footpath after Wp.14

Passing through a bridleway gate, we immediately turn right through another (Wp.14 145M) and in 75 yards downhill, turn left at a marker post. We drop down a fabulous, narrow, terraced footpath, crossing stiles and eventually descending some steps to turn left along a driveway to a road (Wp.15 156M). We turn left and in 35 yards turn right up a tarmac lane, turning left on reaching a high hedge. We soon turn right down a field edge.

Crossing a plank bridge (Wp.16 162M), we turn right along a field edge to cross another plank bridge. Turning right again, along a field edge, we turn left at a T-junction with a track and in 45 yards turn right (Wp.17 178M) along another field edge. We cross a plank bridge, with stile, onto a footpath, which we follow across several stiles and plank bridges. After passing behind a wood, we turn right across a plank bridge (Wp.18 188M), turning half left to diagonally cross a lumpy field, then cross a concrete road by a marker post, maintaining direction across another field.

The Shepherd and Dog

Left at a track, we cross a concrete bridge and soon turn half right over a stile by a field gate. After crossing two fields diagonally, and a stile, we climb up through a kissing gate. Keeping left, we emerge through a gate onto the road at **Fulking**. As we turn right to return to the pub (Wp.1 205M), we pass **The John Ruskin Memorial Fountain**, erected by a grateful brewer (John liked his pint at **The Shepherd and Dog**!). Both **The Shepherd and Dog** and **The Royal Oak** are open all day.

When planning this walk in order to sample the Downs to the east of the **Adur** gap, I wasn't convinced it would be up to the mark! How wrong could I be? It's a wonderful walk, with varying interest and views all the way from start to finish. It also splits conveniently into two shorter walks by means of the **South Downs Way** (**SDW**), for those who may find 9 miles too long.

Even the drive to the start is a scenic revelation. We start from **Beeding Hill** to **Thundersbarrow Hill**, an early settlement, before turning north up a peaceful valley to cross the **SDW**. Descending a stunning terraced track overlooking **Edburton**, we cross the Weald to **South Tottington Farm**, returning towards the Downs through a wood for a steep climb back, finishing on a beautiful footpath round a valley rim.

4 | 3H 40M | 9.1 miles/14.6km | 430m / 430m | ↻ | 🍴 2

Access by car:

From the **Upper Shoreham Road** (which runs between **The Red Lion** roundabout on the A283 and the **Holmbush** roundabout on the A270), turn up **Erringham Road**, following the brown signs for 'Mill Hill' and 'Truleigh Hill'. Take the second turning on the right, **Mill Hill**, following the scenic road for two miles, keeping ahead into the small **Beeding Hill** National Trust car park when the road turns sharp right.

Short Walks

(a) South section. Follow the route to Wp.7 and turn left to take the well signed **SDW** back to **Beeding Hill** (6 miles/9.7km, 2 hours 20 mins).

(b) North section. From the car park entrance turn left, up the tarmac road, on the **SDW**, to pick up the route at Wp.7 (the bottom of the dip after passing the radio masts), turning left through the bridleway gate (7 miles/11.3km, 2 hours 45 mins).

From the car park entrance (Wp.1 0M), we cross the road to a bridleway fingerpost, passing through a bridleway gate and following the left fence line east, up the hill, on **Monarch's Way**, the route taken by King Charles as he fled to France. Our track takes us through two bridleway gates with fine views out to sea, and after passing storage pens we turn right through a steel gate at a T-junction by a marker post (Wp.2 27M).

Turning left at Wp.3

The track leads directly up **Thundersbarrow Hill**, with amazing views over the rolling Downs and coastline as we approach the top. The earthworks are early Iron Age, thought to be a place of refuge rather than a fort; by Roman times it was an extensive farming village.

At the south side we go through a bridleway gate (Wp.3 37M), turning left onto access land, following the left

fence line down to a water trough. We bear right on an indistinct path, down to where scrub meets at a corner, to a path dropping down through the bushes, and cross a low pole barrier. The meandering dog walker's path takes us down through the scrub to bear right, along a hillside, interspersed with grassy wildflower-rich patches, awash with scabious in late summer.

Keeping to the lower slopes, we cross a stile at the bottom, before reaching power lines, and drop down to go over a farm track crossroads (Wp.4 52M) onto a bridleway, up the right side of a gently rising valley.

By a pair of rusting water tanks, we keep ahead to go through a bridleway gate by a fingerpost (Wp.5 63M). In 15 yards we fork left to pass a water trough, and continue on a rising faint grass track, curving over the shoulder of a hill to a bridleway gate at the valley bottom to the left of some trees (Wp.6 73M). Passing through, we steadily climb the peaceful valley bottom, going through a bridleway gate at the top onto the **SDW** (Wp.7 91M), with stunning views across the Weald.

The grass path to Wp.6

For short walk (a) turn left on the **SDW** to return to **Beeding Hill**.

Crossing the **SDW**, we go through another bridleway gate to descend a wonderful steep terraced bridleway which bears left near the bottom, then soon turns right through a bridleway gate to drop down to a road (Wp.8 103M). Turning half left, we cross, going up the concrete driveway of **Aburton Farmhouse**, and continuing ahead between fences, then hedges. 40 yards short of a fingerpost we turn left (Wp.9 114M), following the left hedge line of a field edge.

Looking east from the terraced bridleway towards Devil's Dyke

Crossing a wooden footbridge, we go along another field edge behind a half timbered cottage to a fingerpost by a wooden footbridge (Wp.10 120M). Turning half right diagonally across a field, we enter a wood, going straight through and exiting over a stile. We cross the field, actually an airstrip, to its far left corner, crossing stiles either side of tarmac road (Wp.11 132M).

Turning half right, we diagonally cross two small fields to go over a stile, cross a track and go through a rickety gate. Following the right fence line along a low ridge, with splendid views to the Downs, we cross a stile into the charmingly ramshackle farmyard of **South Tottington Farm**. Passing through a field gate in the centre of the farm (Wp.12 144M), we turn half left down a sometimes muddy track to the bottom of a nearby shallow valley, and then keep ahead up a track between hedges. We go through a gate by a fingerpost, crossing a field, and going over a stile onto an extravagantly wide track through **Tottington Wood**. Emerging through a bridleway gate, along a track between hedges, we pass a cluster of houses, keeping ahead to turn left through a small steel gate by a fingerpost, between high fences, then soon turning right to make our way to the nearby road (Wp.13 165M). **Tottington Manor** bar, restaurant and garden is 100 yards to our left (limited opening hours).

We turn right, then in 50 yards turn left, crossing the road to climb a steep winding bridleway up the scarp slope between fences. Passing through a bridleway gate (Wp.14 180M), we bear left up a meadow on a faint grass track, climbing towards the top of the hill and going through a bridleway gate next to a field gate (Wp.15 189M).

Turning half right, we follow a line of posts towards the sea, with great views across the **Adur** gap and the Downs beyond. At a marker post at the end of a wire fence (Wp.16 194M), we turn right, downhill, to another marker post which soon appears, turning left on an obvious grass track.

Gently descending to a marker post (Wp.17 202M), we keep ahead on a footpath to wind our way round the top of a disused pit and the rim of a beautiful deep valley, the slopes carpeted in cowslips in late spring. The slightly precarious footpath brings us through a kissing gate (Wp.18 214M), dropping down a bank to join a sunken bridleway before going uphill, soon to return us to **Beeding Hill** (Wp.1 221M).

The deep valley in winter

There's not much of it left, but it's an exciting place for kids, both young and old, and it's free! Built in 1073 to guard the **River Adur** gap, when ships could sail right up to the castle, the few bits remaining stand on a massive grassy mound - great place for a picnic, and an adventure!

This fairly short, level walk passes through a short stretch of woodland before descending to the river flood plain for a stroll across pastures. We return down the riverbank to **Bramber High Street**, pass the historic **St Mary's House** (C.1470) and a choice of four places to eat, before walking up to the **Church of St. Nicholas** and back to the castle.

Bramber Castle -the biggest bit left

A walk round the dry moat is a must before you explore the extensive castle mound.

Access by car:
Follow the signs for 'Bramber Castle' from the **Bramber** roundabout on the A283 between **Upper Beeding** and **Steyning**. Park in the free car park.

(Very) Short Walk (30 mins)

Walk round the moat and explore the castle mound.

Turning away from the castle entrance (Wp.1 0M) to the back of the car park, we enter a woodland path which bears slightly right and then almost immediately left at a T-junction, with a bank dropping away to the left. We meander through the trees to arrive at a stile. Crossing into a small paddock, we make for a second stile at the far end which we cross to join a track at a T-junction (Wp.2 5M). Turning right up a slope, we soon pass a fingerpost showing our direction.

Keeping ahead, with garden fences on our left, we reach a stile at the entrance to an open field (Wp.3 12M). With a water-filled ditch below, we follow a raised grassy path until we come to yet another stile (Wp.4 15M).

Turning right, we head for a steel footbridge which takes us over the **River Adur** (Wp.5 17M), continuing straight ahead on an open grassy path, away from the river. After passing a fingerpost to guide us on our way, we reach a water-filled ditch, which we follow ahead until we go over another stile (Wp.6 24M).

The water-filled ditch near Wp.6

Crossing a small field, we squeeze through a person-sized gap by a fingerpost. After a further stile we come to a T-junction (Wp.7 31M) where we turn left on a short stretch of tarmac, changing onto a rough track (still with water on our left) until reaching a stile between two steel gates (Wp.8 37M). We cross an open field on a grassy path, still alongside water, to a double stile next to a steel gate (Wp.9 40M). Climbing over, we turn slightly right, away from the water, to head for an isolated steel gate and stile in the middle of the field (Wp.10 44M).

Here the footpath becomes indistinct, but looking ahead, a raised river bank is visible in the distance running left to right and disappearing into a line of hawthorn bushes which grow on the riverbank. We make for the left end of the bushes, and when we reach the riverbank by a fingerpost (Wp.11 50M), we turn left. At this point the **Adur Gap** between the Downs can be seen, with views to **Chanctonbury Ring** on one side, **Truleigh Hill** to **Devil's Dyke** on the other, with **Lancing College Chapel** visible at the bottom of the gap.

Passing any number of swans on the way, we eventually arrive back at the steel footbridge we crossed earlier. Re-crossing the bridge (Wp.12 75M), we turn left down the opposite bank to reach another stile (Wp.13 78M) where we turn right, away from the river. We follow a grassy and sometimes moist path until we eventually come to a stile, just to the right of a white house, at **Bramber High Street** (Wp.14 85M). We cross the road and turn right, passing historic **St Mary's House** and **The Castle Inn**. When we reach **The Old Tollgate Hotel** (Wp.15 90M, and the best carvery in Sussex) we cross the road to climb the steps to **St. Nicholas' Church** and the castle car park (Wp.1 93M).

22 CHANCTONBURY RING

The distinctive outline of **Chanctonbury Ring**, the fifth highest point on the Downs, is a classic distant feature of many walks in this book, despite the decimation of the 200 year old beech trees crowning the top in the 1987 hurricane.

We set off on an underdown track, once the road from **Steyning** to **Washington**, turning up through the wooded scarp slope to climb to the **Ring**. After following the **South Downs Way** with uplifting views to the sea, we start our return overlooking **Steyning** and through the striking woods around **Pepperscoombe**. We descend to a fine level footpath, parallel to the **Downs**, with views of the **Elizabethan Wiston House**, finally passing through **Great Barn Farm**.

| 3 | 3¼ H | 8.3 miles/13.4km | ⛰ | 320m ↕ 320m | ↻ | 0 |

Short Walks
(a) 3.7miles/6km (1hr 40m). Follow the route to Wp.6 and turn left down **Wiston Bostal** on a popular track to return to the start.

(b) 6miles/9.7km (2hr 15m). From the car park turn towards the Downs and keep ahead up the well worn **Wiston Bostal** to emerge at the top by Wp.6, turning left to continue the route.

Access by car:
Follow the signs to **Chanctonbury** from the A283 between **Steyning** and **Washington**. Park in the car park on the left 0.7 miles from the A283.

From the car park entrance (Wp.1 0M), we head towards the **Downs**, turning right by a fingerpost to pass a cottage on a bridleway and skirting a field before entering a wood. Our track undulates along the edge of the wood, the scarp slope above still littered with the debris of the 1987 hurricane.

We pass through a vintage steel gate, following a dry path through trees to the left to avoid the sometimes muddy main track which we soon re-join. Passing through another vintage gate onto a terraced track brings us to a T-junction by a marker post (Wp.2 18M), where we bear left. We keep right at a bridleway junction along the wood edge before the track winds up the slope.

Passing a marker post, we eventually emerge into a field through a bridleway gate (Wp.3 33M) crossing ahead to another gate.

The north side of the Ring

Going through, we turn sharp left onto the **SDW** for 70 yards before forking left to go through a bridleway gate (Wp.4 37M) and climbing up through disused pit workings to pass through another gate. We head to the left side of the crown of the hill and make for a fine dew pond.

Dropping down to a nearby bridleway gate (Wp.5 49M) we turn left, passing a round barrow as we approach the **Ring**.

Chanctonbury Ring was an Iron-Age fort, a Roman temple and a Roman and Saxon burial ground. Steeped in mystery and legend - should you manage to run round the Ring seven times on a moonless night, without falling over or stopping, the Devil will appear with a bowl of soup (dread to think what flavour it might be!).

Looking towards a snow-capped Devil's Dyke

A circuit around the **Ring** yields superb views in all directions before we turn east to join the nearby flint track of the **SDW**, and pass through a bridleway gate by a cattle grid. At a fingerpost crossroads (Wp.6 69M), (For short walk (a) we turn left down **Wiston** **Bostal** to return to the start. For short walk (b) we turn left to join the route on the **SDW**), we continue ahead on the **SDW** for some time, passing two marker posts at T-junctions and enjoying uplifting views to the sea. Immediately before a 5-way crossroads (Wp.7 100M), we turn sharp left, onto a grass path.

Turning right at a T-junction by a seat (Wp.8 106M) we go through a bridleway gate with marvellous views over **Steyning** and towards **Devil's Dyke**. We descend a terraced grass path, forking left by a marker post to go through a bridleway gate at the edge of a wood and down to a marker post towards the bottom (Wp.9 117M). Turning hard left into the wood we take the right fork, signed in yellow 'Steyning Nature Trail', passing through a kissing gate on a clear woodland path around the attractive **Pepperscoombe**. We pass through two kissing gates before turning hard left onto a wide rising path at a junction by a marker post (Wp.10 139M). Half way up the slope we fork right on an unmarked path (Wp11 141M), winding up through a wood to turn right at a T-junction.

At the next T-junction (Wp.12 147M), we turn right, keeping to the main downward track, eventually emerging along a field edge, then between hedges to turn left up some steps by a footpath fingerpost (Wp.13 150M).

The footpath follows field edges with views up to the **Downs** until, in a field corner, we turn left and in 50 yards turn right by a fingerpost (Wp.14 163M). Crossing a stream and two stiles we follow the field edges to a track between hedges. We soon bear left on a tarmac road (Wp.15 169M) with views of the nearby **Wiston House**, reputed to be the first place in England where coffee was imbibed. Passing under an estate footbridge, we continue ahead, leaving the tarmac road to cross a scaffold stile onto a track.

A distant Chanctonbury Ring from near Wp.13

We pass through **Great Barn Farm**, an old wooden granary still standing on its mushroom shaped *steddle stones* (rats cannot climb up and spoil the grain), and some unusual horned cattle. Going over a stile by a steel gate to a T-junction, we turn right to return to the car park (Wp.1 186M).

A visit to nearby **Steyning** is recommended, with wonderful buildings in the **High Street** and especially **Church Street**, a selection of pubs and tea rooms and a small local museum. In 1885 at **The White Horse Inn**, as Steyning Fire Brigade was holding its annual supper there, the Inn caught fire and was gutted, (as indeed were the firemen!).

23 CISSBURY RING

Neolithic flint mines produced the tools to enable the clearance of downland trees for the introduction of agriculture. **Cissbury** was a major production centre. These flint implements were traded over a wide area, along the same tracks we walk today. The impressive Iron Age hill fort, the largest on the South Downs, was constructed around 350 BC, enclosing an area of 60 acres with two ramparts separated by a ditch with entrances to the south and east.

We climb to enter the east gate of the **Cissbury Ring**, taking a complete circuit of the inner rampart before sampling the mid slopes of the undulating South Downs, passing an attractive flint farm and returning along the lovely flanks of **Lychpole Hill**.

Access by car:
Travelling north on the A24 towards **Findon**, take the third turning on the right after the main shopping parade, turning up **Central Avenue**. Travelling south on the A24, take the third turning on the left after the '40mph' signs on the outskirts of **Worthing**, turn up **Central Avenue**, and go right at the top, parking on the road by a fingerpost immediately on the left.

Short Walks
(a) Cissbury Ring, ideal for a family picnic. Follow the route to Wp.5, and then skip forward picking up the route at the next mention of Wp.5 to return (1 hour 20 mins, 3½ miles/5.6km).

(b) With alternative parking at the car park near Wp.5 (may be full at popular times), accessed through **Findon** village centre on the narrow road passing **Nepcote Green**. A walk over the gently undulating downland, returning along the slopes of **Lychpole Hill**. Starting and finishing at Wp.5 (2 hours, 5.4 miles/8.7km).

From the fingerpost (Wp.1 0M), we pass between posts, turning left and then right to follow the right hedge line up the meadow edge. In the top corner we enter a wood, keeping ahead on a rising path, soon turning right and then left to join the footpath, which steeply follows the left fence line up the wood edge.

At a marker post we bear left, eventually crossing a stile by a gate and keeping ahead to go through a bridleway gate between two steel gates (Wp.2 21M). We descend a chalky track, crossing two attractive shallow valleys, to bear left at a T-junction. We soon fork left, on a grass path, towards the causeway entrance to **Cissbury Ring**. Passing through a kissing gate (Wp.3 40M), we cross the causeway, turning left up some steps to the top of the inner bank to start our circuit around the Ring.

Soon after dipping down to cross the south entrance, as we approach the west side, we can see a number of depressions on our right - the tell tale signs of Neolithic flint mine shafts.

The north-west side of Cissbury Ring

The scale of the fortifications soon becomes clear from the towering ramparts of the western side, as does the fortification's totally dominant position. We enjoy fantastic views, then continue along the top to return to the east entrance, passing through the kissing gate (Wp.3 65M) and turning half left to another nearby kissing gate.

Passing through, we bear left to descend a chalky, terraced track, bearing right by a fingerpost (Wp.4 71M) to drop down a grass path through scrub, leaving the environs of the **Cissbury Ring** through a bridleway gate (Wp.5 73M).

Keeping ahead on a chalky bridleway, we pass the small car park area (the start point for short walk (b)). At a crossroads by a marker post (Wp.6 78M), we turn right, following the right fence line on the gently undulating, open path of **Monarch's Way**. We eventually arrive at a 6-way junction (Wp.7 101M), turning hard right on a farm track, soon becoming a grass track with occasional hawthorn tree tunnels as we meander down the shallow valley floor. The high ground to our left is the site of the substantial Bronze, Iron Age and Roman settlement of **Park Brow**, but on inaccessible farmland.

At a T-junction by a dry dew pond, we turn left (Wp.8 119M), on a wide track. As the track splits, we fork right, turning sharp right at the top of the slope (Wp.9 128M) and going down a surfaced track to pass a large barn. We wind through the very attractive flint and brick **Lychpole Farm**, following a concrete road and passing several large barns.

Lychpole Farm

As the road bears left, we turn right (Wp.10 138M), passing two modern barns onto a stony track. Just before a bridleway gate and field gate, we leave the track, turning right on a grass path and passing through a nearby bridleway gate (Wp.11 145M). Turning half right, we join a slightly terraced track running along the top of a long, organic meadow, on the slopes of **Lychpole Hill**.

Our path becomes strikingly attractive, with rolling downland views to our right. We pass a dew pond, hidden by brambles on our left, before going through a bridleway gate (Wp.12 168M). Keeping ahead, we pass through another gate, taking the lower path following the right fence line.

Eventually we pass through a bridleway gate, turning left onto a wide flint track joining from our right (Wp.13 177M).

We soon step up onto the bank of the right fence line for a superior path to return to Wp.5 (183M). Turning left, through the bridleway gate, we bear right following the right fence line to pass through a bridleway gate on a grass path. We fork left on a narrow path, gently snaking up and over the shoulder of the hill.

Soon after passing a kissing gate on our left, we turn half right at a grass crossroads (Wp.14 193M), on a wide grass path, dropping down and passing through a kissing gate in the hedge line below.

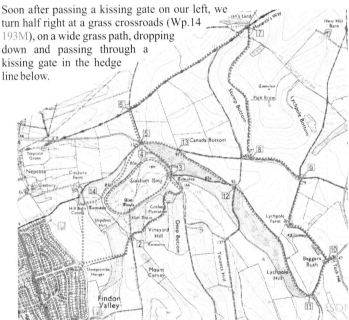

We turn half left, diagonally crossing a meadow on a grass path, passing through a gap in the trees and keeping ahead to return to the start (Wp.1 205M). **The Gun**, in the centre of **Findon** village, is recommended as the nearest watering hole, open all day.

Sullington is a hidden delight, off the beaten track. Little has changed for centuries - a church and farm have been here for 900 years. In contrast, **Storrington** is a fairly large village with an interesting range of shops and pubs. **Storrington** folk were once the butt of a Sussex joke; it was said they were so stupid they had to go outside to look at a pond to see if it was raining!

Starting from **Storrington Church**, we pass a monastery and go across some delightful fields before the fairly stiff wooded climb to the top of the Downs to be rewarded with stunning views. We pass the source of the 'mighty' **River Stor** and climb back up a delightful valley for a glimpse of **Chanctonbury Ring** before we return via **Sullington** and along the banks of the 'river' to **Storrington**.

Access by car: If approaching **Storrington** from the west, on the A283, **Church Lane** is on the right in the middle of the village. If approaching from the east, **Church Lane** is on the left, with roadside parking in the vicinity of the church.

> **Short Walk**
> A delightful walk; follow the route to Wp.9, turning hard left, downhill, to follow the bridleway past a barn and on down to **Sullington Church** to continue the route back from the church steps at Wp.14 (1 hour 55 mins, 5 miles/8km).

Starting up the steps at the north-east corner of the church (Wp.1 0M), we go through the churchyard on a footpath and over a fingerpost crossroads, keeping ahead to pass five isolated gravestones and go through a kissing gate. We head towards the left field corner, go through another kissing gate and pass the monastery. At a T-junction (Wp.2 5M), we turn left uphill, glancing to our right to see a rest garden with a shrine to the Virgin Mary, and bear right at the top into **Kithurst Lane**.

At the top of a rise we keep ahead, then bear left onto a footpath between fences by a telegraph pole (Wp.3 9M), to the left of a gravel drive. Almost unexpectedly, we soon emerge into open countryside, with the tree-clad Downs towering ahead of us. Following the right fence line, we cross two wooden footbridges and emerge into a field. Keeping ahead to pass a lone oak tree by a fingerpost, we follow the right hedge/fence line, on a rising grass track, passing blackberry bushes laden with fruit in late summer. We cross a stile in the corner (Wp.4 27M), soon turning left in front of an appealing stone built cottage and turning right, up the cottage driveway.

At a junction with a bridleway, we keep ahead, uphill towards the Downs, turning right at the first marker post. Our path climbs the steep wooded scarp slope up a sunken bridleway; we keep to the higher path on the right whenever there is a choice. At a crossroads marker post near the top (Wp.5 55M), we turn left, passing several round barrows to our left, and **Kithurst Hill** trig point, before going through a bridleway gate. We follow the right fence line, as stunning views open out seaward, and across the disused pit workings to

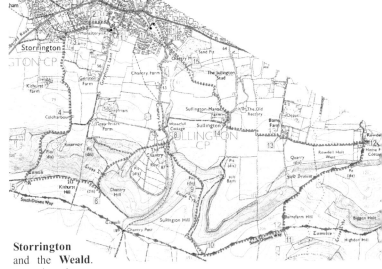

Storrington

and the **Weald**.

Dropping down to a finger post (Wp.6 70M), we turn hard left, on an attractive terraced path, descending **Chantry Hill**. At a marker post halfway down the hill (Wp.7 77M), we fork right onto a footpath, bearing right on reaching the bottom to pass through a gate. In 30 yards we go through a steel gate, following the left fence line of a field to go through another gate, and passing farm buildings to arrive at a T-junction with **Chantry Lane** (Wp.8 89M).

The terraced path from Wp.6

Climbing to Wp.9

The spring-fed lake opposite is the source of the **River Stor**, hence 'Storrington'. Turning right, we soon fork left up a bridleway opposite the imposing **Chantry House** for a steady ascent back to the heights. Passing through a bridleway gate we keep ahead, emerging to climb to the top of the left bank for the best path. We go through a field gate and climb to a marker post (Wp.9 107M).

For the short walk turn hard left, downhill, following the bridleway down to **Sullington Farm** and church to resume the route.

We keep right, up a rising bridleway track, passing through the attractive grassy mounds of disused pit workings onto a terraced track. We pass a fingerpost, keeping right, round the field edge, eventually joining the main uphill flint track by a marker post. Passing through two steel gates by cattle grids, we turn left onto the **South Downs Way (SDW)** (Wp.10 121M), tracking the left fence line uphill. Keeping ahead through a gate by an overgrown cattle grid, the distinctive **Chanctonbury Ring** comes into view, with **Cissbury Ring** away to our right. On reaching a fingerpost at a T-junction we turn left on the **SDW** 'alternative route' (Wp.11 135M) to drop down **Barnsfarm Hill**, eventually joining a tarmac road and passing a cottage and **Home Farm**. At a road T-junction we keep ahead, immediately turning left onto a bridleway between tall bushes (Wp.12 158M) which takes us between fences to a clear track ahead between arable fields, paralleling the Downs.

Sullington Church

Crossing a farm track, we keep ahead through a bridleway gate, passing south around **Barns Farm** and turning left at a fingerpost (Wp.13 175M). Going through gates either side of a racehorse gallop, we follow the field edge round until we eventually turn right through a steel gate, passing farm buildings and climbing the churchyard steps (Wp.14 185M). **Sullington Church** is a cracker; a very tranquil churchyard with a fine interior dating back to the Saxons, (apart from the incongruous internal glass doors). A peek over the wall near the church door reveals the **Manor House** and a glimpse of a very fine tithe barn (restored 1685).

Peeking over the wall ...

Returning down the churchyard steps, we keep ahead down a tarmac road to a T-junction where we turn left, then in 20 yards turn right to cross a stile by a steel gate. We bear right by a charming flint byre onto a wide grass drove which soon bends left to a stile by a steel gate. Crossing, we turn right then left, following round the field edge to a fingerpost, bearing half right diagonally across a field to cross a stile in the far corner (Wp.15 201M). We go over a bridge, bearing left, to take a winding woodland path which emerges into **Chantry Lane** (Wp.16 207M). Crossing diagonally, we go through a steel safety barrier, then through an excellent children's play park. Exiting through a gate we bear left, cross a road and follow the right bank of the 'mighty' **River Stor**. At a gravel path by an information board, we turn left, crossing the river and turning right along a residential road (Wp.17 216M). The footway takes us to the right of a house at a 'no cycling' sign, soon emerging into **Storrington High Street**. We can turn right to visit **The Anchor Inn**, and left for **The New Moon** or the fish and chip shop. To return to the start we turn left, taking the next left again into **Church Street** to arrive back at the church (Wp.1 225M). One final oddity; at the corner of **Browns Lane**, is a fantastic carved Indian mahogany door, apparently a copy of a famous door in Lahore.

Harrow Hill is one of Britain's earliest industrial sites; there are 160 flint mine shafts on the hill, dating from around 4000 B.C. There is also an Iron-Age earthwork enclosure, and it is possibly the site of a heathen Saxon shrine. No surprise then, that legend has it that **Harrow Hill** was the last place where fairies were seen in England!

We start high up at **Chantry Post** to widely circle **Harrow Hill**, passing through a magical glade, the woods of **Michelgrove Park** and crossing the ancient settlement of **Barpham Hill**, all the while with ever changing views, with one last surprise on the way back.

3   3H   8.2 miles/13.2km   320m / 320m   0

Access by car:
From the A283 on the eastern edge of **Storrington**, follow the signs for **Chantry Lane** which climbs, at times like a roller coaster, for 1.6 miles to **Chantry Post** car park.

Short Walk
A smaller circuit of **Harrow Hill**. Follow the route to Wp.3, cross the stile and turn right to cross fields around the south west shoulder of **Harrow Hill**. We turn right at a T-junction near **Lee Farm** to follow the bridleway on a steady climb back to **Chantry Post**. (4.4 miles/7.1km, 1 hour 25 mins)

Long walk option
Link to Walk 26 at Wp.10*, turning left on the **SDW** to **Kithurst Hill** car park, for a 15 mile 'figure of eight' day walk

Facing south, we go through a steel bridleway gate beside an **Angmering Park Estate** field gate (Wp.1 0M), turning half left diagonally across an arable field and making for a bridleway gate in the fence line below. We maintain a diagonal direction to a left fence line which we follow to gently descend towards **Blackpatch**, surrounded by rolling **Downs**, with **Harrow Hill**, pock marked with flint mine depressions, to our right.

The bridleway gate, Harrow Hill beyond

Passing through a field gate we turn half right, guided by a fingerpost, on a faint grass track making for a meaningless bridleway gate in the middle of the field. A more obvious path then takes us through a gate in the far right corner, turning right onto a footpath to follow the fingerpost direction (Wp.2 28M). Going downhill we cross a stile at the valley bottom, making for and crossing a stile at the wood edge opposite.

We follow the path, which soon opens out into a magical hillside glade (see picture on the next page), alive with insects and the sweet smell of wild thyme in the summer.

The magical hillside glade

If the fairies are still here, this haven of tranquillity must be their playground.

Leaving the glade across a stile, we turn right following the fence line around a field, and crossing a stile to emerge onto a tarmac estate road, where we turn left (Wp.3 41M).

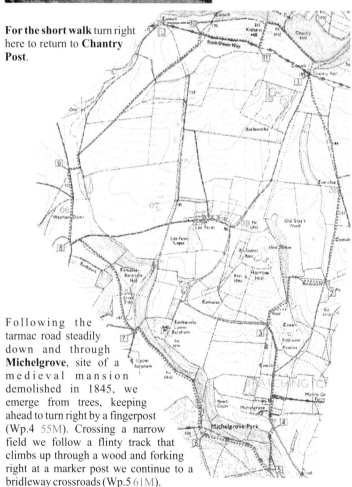

For the short walk turn right here to return to **Chantry Post**.

Following the tarmac road steadily down and through **Michelgrove**, site of a medieval mansion demolished in 1845, we emerge from trees, keeping ahead to turn right by a fingerpost (Wp.4 55M). Crossing a narrow field we follow a flinty track that climbs up through a wood and forking right at a marker post we continue to a bridleway crossroads (Wp.5 61M).

Turning right onto a wide, sometimes muddy, forest track, we pass a T-junction before going right at a bridleway crossroads (Wp.6 72M).

We turn right again at a T-junction, keeping ahead through a small clearing before emerging from the trees as the track follows a field edge to go through a gate. We bear left along a terraced track with views across **Lower Barpham** and the surrounding **Downs** across to **Harrow Hill**.

Lower Barpham and Harrow Hill

Going through a steel gate, we curve left and uphill to a marker post just beyond a flint track (Wp.7 93M).

We go right and uphill on a stony track to pass through a bridleway gate beside a double field gate. Following the track, now grass, we cross the ancient settlement site of **Barpham Hill** to go through a field gate and a small copse before crossing another meadow.

Leaving through a field gate, we turn left, uphill, on a track between wire fences, then go right at a T-junction onto a concrete track. In 30 yards we fork right at a fingerpost (Wp.8 111M) to follow the right fence line downhill. After passing through a bridleway gate we turn right by a fingerpost, through another bridleway gate (Wp.9 121M) and cross a small field to the north end of a copse.

After turning left through a bridleway gate, we follow the fence line before forking half right at a fingerpost to cross a large arable field. At a fence gap by a fingerpost we keep to the left fork to cross another field, turning to enjoy the view down to **Arundel Castle** in the distance.

Hulk of the WWII tank

Going round a steel barrier gate to a marker post, we keep left of the hedge line, and as we approach a copse we pass the rusting bullet-riddled hulk of a WWII tank used as target practice before the D-Day landings. Passing through the copse, we keep ahead at a bridleway crossroads, turning right at the next crossroads onto the **SDW** (Wp.10 152M)

*(turning left here to the nearby **Kithurst Hill** car park will link with Walk 26).

At the top of a rise by a fingerpost (Wp.11 169M), we turn left on a gently rising path to go through a bridleway gate, turning right to be rewarded with views across **Storrington** and the **Weald**. Following the right fence line we pass through a bridleway gate to emerge onto a road. Crossing, we scramble up the bank onto a short path up to the car park (Wp.1 182M). **Storrington** has several pubs open all day for refreshments.

This attractive route heads west along the **South Downs Way** with superb views across the upper **Arun** valley, before dropping down a stunning footpath and on to the ruin of **Rackham Mill**. We pass through a delightful wood, and enter the 16th century **Parham Park** with its Elizabethan manor house, emerging at **Cootham** near **The Crown Inn**. A sharp, wooded climb takes us back to the start.

3	2H 35M	6½ miles/10½km	250m 250m		2

Access by car:
Take the B2139 from **Storrington** past a flint cottage on a fairly sharp right hand bend; we turn left after a road junction sign. We follow the narrow road to the top of the Downs, turning right into **Kithurst Hill** car park. If approaching from **Amberley**, after passing some farm cottages on the left, turn right 200 yards after a road junction sign.

Extension
Can be linked to walk 25 for an interesting and varied, figure of eight, day walk 14.5 miles, 23.3 kilometres.

We head to the west end of the car park (Wp.1 0M) and cross a shallow ditch to join the **South Downs Way** (**SDW**). Just after a small copse, we keep right at a fingerpost (Wp.2 12M), still on the **SDW**. On reaching a crossroads fingerpost on our left (Wp.3 25M), we turn right through a bridleway gate.

... wonderful views across the Weald ...

The path veers left then right, to begin one of the most stunning descents on the Downs with wonderful views across the **Weald** and the upper **Arun** valley. We go through a bridleway gate, keeping straight ahead, down on a lightly wooded path to emerge from another bridleway gate onto a busy road (Wp.4 40M).

Across it, we turn left along the narrow verge until we reach a T-junction, then go right to follow the sign for **Rackham**.

After passing **Rackham** farmhouse we descend through a tree 'tunnel', and just after the second cottage on our left, we find a footpath fingerpost (Wp.5 49M) where we turn left, following the footpath between gardens and crossing two stiles to enter a meadow. We head for a lone, large tree on the flood plain below, and as we come over the brow of the hill we make for a stile ahead and cross onto a road (Wp.6 54M) where we turn left and uphill, going right onto a footpath just past the 30 mph signs (Wp.7 60M).

We take a diagonal path down a sloping arable field with views across the **Arun** flood plain - it's even well worth getting your feet damp after rain to see

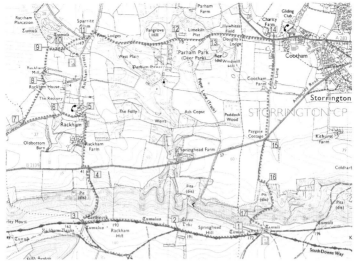

Looking back from Wp.8

the vast lake of **Amberley Wild Brooks** and the wildfowl. On the far side of the field we cross two small wooden footbridges and a small meadow to reach and cross a stile (Wp.8 68M) before going over a wooden footbridge and following the path alongside a wire fence.

Over another stile and a footbridge, our path now winds through delightful woodland, emerging at a stile by the disused **Rackham Mill**. Skirting the mill and passing a fingerpost, we cross a stile by a steel gate and continue along the edge of the flood plain towards the woods. After crossing a footbridge to join a T-junction (Wp.9 75M), we turn right onto a track.

Parham Park

Past a house on our right, we turn left at a footpath marker post (Wp.10 79M) to follow a lovely, winding path through the woods, emerging at a road (Wp.11 83M) to turn right then almost immediately left, onto the road signposted 'Wiggonholt'.

At a pair of gatehouses at the entrance to **Parham Park**, we enter through a cream kissing gate - it's supposedly a deer park, though I've yet to see a deer there, not even a dropping! We follow the private road past a lake and the back of **Parham House** to reach a T-junction (Wp.12 100M).

This fine house is well worth a visit, as is the church, which has the height of luxury for the Lord of the Manor, a pew with his own personal fireplace!

We go straight ahead on a grass path, by a 'Footpath to Cootham' sign. When the path rejoins the tarmac road (Wp.13 105M), we continue ahead to leave the park through a kissing gate at the gatehouse and join the busy A283, where we turn right, along the footway. At **Clay Lane**, we have the options of continuing ahead to **The Crown Inn** for refreshments, or of turning right (Wp. 14 116M) to follow a quiet road towards the distant Downs. On reaching a T-junction we cross the busy road, turning right along the verge. We turn left at a fingerpost just past the flint cottage (Wp.15 128M) and pass through a bridleway gate onto a gently rising track.

As we reach woodland, we turn left by a fingerpost, following the track up the slope. By a fingerpost to the right of a steel gate (Wp.16 135M) we fork right uphill, along the edge of a conifer plantation to follow the steeply rising sunken path until, nearing the top, the path turns sharp left at a fingerpost (Wp.17 151M). We climb to go through a bridleway gate into a small 'organic' meadow, following the fence line to another bridleway gate. Going through the gate, we turn half right up the slope to **Kithurst Hill** car park, turning right to return to the start (Wp.1 155M).

Burpham is an ancient place; there is evidence of Britons, Romans and Saxons. The church is remarkable for its amazing interior, particularly the chancel chalk vaulting and the leper window, through which the priest blessed victims in the Middle Ages. But the most fascinating part of the village is the Saxon figure-of-eight fortified promontory, believed to have been built by Alfred the Great around 910 AD, as a defence against Danish Viking raiders. At 700 yards long and covering 22 acres, it has a massive earth rampart at the landward end.

From within the promontory, we drop down across fields to take an amazing terraced footpath overlooking the fort before heading for the hills. Our return passes the **Lepers' Path** to take in views across the **Arun** valley to **Bignor Hill**, completing our walk through **Wepham** and **Burpham** villages.

Access by car:
Follow the signs for **Burpham** from the A27, just east of **Arundel Station**. In 2.6 miles turn left at **The George and Dragon** pub to the free car park.

Short Walk Option
Turn left at Wp.11, cross the racehorse gallop, and cross a stile into a field, following the fence line up and turning right at the top onto a road up towards **Home Farm**. When the concrete road turns right go left over a stile onto a wide grass track to reach a fingerpost at Wp.15. Turn left to re-join the route. (4.1 miles/6.6km).

Walking back towards the car park entrance (Wp.1 0M), we turn left to pass **Burpham** village hall. After following the fence line to a children's play park we turn left over a stile, heading across the field to a stile opposite (Wp.2 4M).

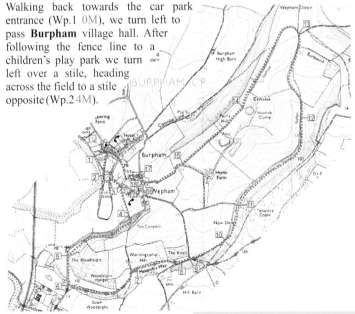

As we cross the stile as we drop down the side of the fort to join a road below, keeping ahead on the right footway. After passing a thatched cottage set back from the road, we turn right over a stile by a telegraph pole (Wp.3 10M). After crossing another stile by the thatched cottage, we turn half left onto an almost invisible path across a meadow to head for a stile which soon appears in the distant hedge. Crossing this stile (Wp.4 16M) and a road, we climb several steps by a fingerpost to enter a wood, soon reaching a T-junction where we turn right through an area of neglected coppicing. We leave the wood over a stile onto a terraced path, and in 50 yards the Saxon fort comes into view on our right.

King Alfred's Fort

The fort would have been largely surrounded by the estuary of the **River Arun** before the days of land reclamation. It's clearly in a commanding position overlooking the river, particularly as the main channel used to flow down the west edge, perhaps with a harbour on the east side nearest to us.

Crossing a stile into a meadow, we make for another stile in the far right corner which we cross to drop down to the road (Wp.5 34M) where we turn left. Near the top of a slope we turn left by a barrier gate and fingerpost (Wp.6 38M), onto an attractive terraced woodland bridleway. Passing through a wooden gate, we follow the path as it drops down towards the valley floor, ignoring the fingerpost on our right and heading for another, 150 yards ahead on the valley floor (Wp.7 53M). Keeping along the right side of the valley floor, the track passes through a wooden gate where we bear right and immediately left (Wp.8 62M).

At a fingerpost (Wp.9 64M) we bear right, following the bridleway as it swings left. Reaching a bridleway T-junction (Wp.10 73M), we turn left and soon bear right through a steel field gate into **Angmering Park Estate** to follow a racehorse gallop along the right side of the gently rising valley.

Short Walk Option
Turn left at the footpath crossroads by a fingerpost (Wp.11 83M) for the short cut via **Home Farm**, rejoining the route at Wp.15.

We continue up the right side of the valley, eventually passing through a steel field gate (Wp.12 106M); there's evidence of field systems and earthworks all around, particularly on our right on the slopes of **Barpham Hill**. We go through a bridleway gate onto a track between fences, to arrive at a junction where we keep ahead on a concrete track. By a fingerpost at the end of the concrete section (Wp.13 120M), we bear left onto a gently rising track.

A fingerpost on our left marks a footpath that forks right, down the slope. This is known as **Lepers' Path** – in the Middle Ages there was a leper colony high on the Downs near **Lee Farm**, and this path was used by the afflicted to get to

Burpham Church. However, we fortunates continue ahead to **Norfolk Clump** copse at the top of a rise (Wp.14 126M) from where we bear slightly right to descend on a grass track, following the fence line on our right, then crossing a stile by a double steel gate to continue following the fence line, now to our left. There are spectacular views ahead and right of the **Arun Valley**, **Bignor Hill** and **Arundel Castle**, and of the village of **Burpham** below.

At a fingerpost (Wp.15 149M) we bear right then left to cross a stile, descending on a grass path to cross another stile. On reaching a T-junction with a road (Wp.16 157M) we turn right at the village of **Wepham**. Going left down a concrete road between flint cottages (Wp.17 159M), we pass to the right of a flint barn and turn right over a stile at a marker post (Wp.18 161M).

Burpham, looking across to Bignor Hill

We follow a grass footpath between gardens, cross a stile, and turn left over a meadow, heading for and crossing a stile on the far side, then dropping down a long flight of steps to make for a stile in the far corner of the field.

The George and Dragon, from the church

Emerging onto a road, we turn right uphill to turn left at a T-junction. As we reach **The George and Dragon** (circa 1736) we turn left, passing through a gap in the fort's landward defensive rampart to the car park (Wp.1 170M).

A visit to **Burpham Church** is recommended (entrance opposite the pub) to see its fine interior.

28 ARUNDEL PARK & AMBERLEY

A long but rewarding walk, encompassing a variety of landscapes: river, lake, woodland, downland, flood plain, thatched village, and even castles.

We start down the bank of the **River Arun**, passing **Swanbourne Lake** before climbing the unspoilt Downs of **Arundel Park**. Descending to the wooded riverbank and across the flood plain, we pass beneath the walls of **Amberley Castle** into the picturesque village. After a break, perhaps, at **The Black Horse**, we climb to the high Downs before descending to pass through a swampy wood on a winding, dry raised path, crossing the river to return to **The Black Rabbit**.

| 4 | 4H 25M | 11.7 miles/18.8km | 400m 400m | 3 |

Access by car: From the centre of **Arundel** follow the brown signs towards the 'WWT Wildfowl Trust'. Go past the WWT entrance, turning right in ¼ mile to pass in front of **The Black Rabbit** into the car park beyond. If not intending to take refreshment at the pub, alternative roadside parking is available near **Swanbourne Lake**, near the stone bridge, in which case, start the walk from Wp.3.

Short Walks

(a) A delightful walk through **Arundel Park**, along riverbanks and the flood plain edge. Follow the route to Wp.8 turning right along the beautiful terraced bridleway above the river, following marker and fingerposts to rejoin the route at the middle gate at Wp.24. (1hour 50mins, 4.8 miles/7.7km)

(b) Alternative parking by **The Black Horse** at **Amberley**, for a fine village, downland and river walk. Starting from Wp.13, follow the route to Wp.24, keeping ahead, immediately turning right onto the bridleway, passing the Victorian brick barn before turning left to follow the fingerposts to re-join the route at Wp.8 by the kissing gate. (3 hours 5 mins, 8.3 miles/13.4km)

We walk back past the pub, keeping left at the car park entrance (Wp.1 0M) before turning left at the end of a post and rail fence onto the raised riverbank towards **Arundel**. Passing the wildfowl reserve on our right, we go through a kissing gate by a sluice, turning right across a stile (Wp.2 8M). We follow an attractive waterside path, with views to **Arundel Castle**, turning right across a footbridge, then left down steps before climbing more steps to a road by the stone bridge.

Turning right, we soon cross the road to go through a gap in the low fence by a fingerpost (Wp.3 15M). Keeping ahead to a path between fences, we enter **Arundel Park** onto a stunning, terraced path, running above the south side of **Swanbourne Lake**. Soon after passing the fantastically twisted roots of a beech tree, we keep left to cross a stile (Wp.4 32M), keeping ahead on a grass path along the wildflower-rich valley bottom, to join a track from our right. At a T-junction, we turn right and immediately bear left up a steep footpath, climbing with a valley on either side. We cross a stile (Wp.5 40M) and continue up a large, organic meadow. Passing a pair of isolated trees, we keep ahead to a stand of six holm oaks and cross a stile, soon linking with a track joining from our right at a wood edge. At the end of the wood we bear right, in the fingerpost direction, with amazing views opening out across the **Arun Valley** as we drop down to cross a stile by a gate in the fence ahead (Wp.6 58M). We follow the chalky track downhill, keeping on the right bank as long as possible, turning right at a T-junction by a fingerpost and soon turning left at another fingerpost (Wp.7 65M), following the right fence line downhill through a wood edge.

Looking east from the chalky track

Towards the bottom our path follows a high, flint, estate wall, soon passing through a fine steel kissing gate onto a bridleway (Wp.8 70M), with the pungent aroma of a carpet of ramsons in spring.

For short walk (a) turn right at Wp.8 along a beautiful, terraced woodland path, following the fingerposts with the wood edge on the left. Eventually turn right after passing a modern barn, and soon pass a fine Victorian brick barn, turning left at a road and immediately right to the middle gate to rejoin the route at Wp.24.

We turn left along the attractive wooded path running above the **River Arun**. At a fingerpost by a steel gate (Wp.9 87M) we turn left uphill, passing some fine old cottages of **Houghton** village to a T-junction with a road (Wp.10 90M). To the left is **The George and Dragon Inn** (King Charles II reputedly stayed here before fleeing to France). We turn right then immediately left down the road signed 'Bury'. At a fingerpost, we turn right through a gate, joining the **SDW** (Wp.11 94M) and crossing a field to turn right through another gate. We follow the field edge to go through yet another gate onto the raised riverbank.

Turning right, we cross a large footbridge over the **River Arun** before turning left along the riverbank towards the village of **Bury**. Opposite the village, by what once was the ferry linking the villages of **Bury** and **Amberley**, we turn right by a marker post (Wp.12 107M) towards the distant **Amberley Castle**. Crossing a water meadow, we go over an isolated stile by a gate, keeping ahead to cross a ditch and another stile between gates.

The thatched cottage where we turn left

We carefully cross stiles either side of a railway line before passing below the impressive, towering walls of **Amberley Castle** (not actually a castle; once a palace for the Bishop of Chichester, fortified in 1377 and now a rather expensive hotel). Joining a tarmac road, we pass the church to enter the pretty village of **Amberley**, with its many thatched cottages. Until recent times the village was virtually surrounded by water, particularly in winter; **Amberley** folk were said to

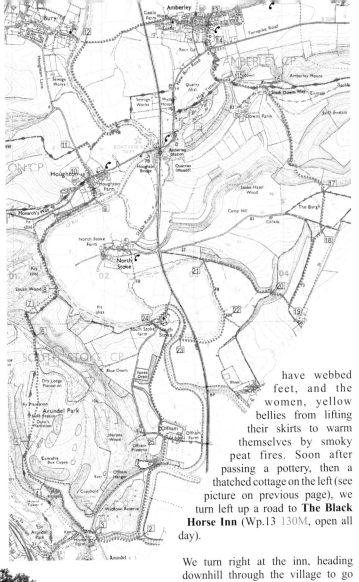

have webbed feet, and the women, yellow bellies from lifting their skirts to warm themselves by smoky peat fires. Soon after passing a pottery, then a thatched cottage on the left (see picture on previous page), we turn left up a road to **The Black Horse Inn** (Wp.13 130M, open all day).

We turn right at the inn, heading downhill through the village to go over a busy road junction (Wp.14 135M) and climb up **Mill Lane**, keeping ahead as we join with the **SDW** at a road junction. At a post and rail barrier by a gate, we turn left (Wp.15 144M) up a steep slope and through a bridleway gate. A farm track joins from the right shortly before we pass through a bridleway gate by a steel gate. We fork right (Wp.16 153M) onto a track curving round the shoulder of a hill, soon keeping right

Ascending the track towards Wp.17

to follow the right fence line. Through a bridleway gate, still following the right fence, we come to a track curving down to the valley bottom.

Turning right through a bridleway gate, we ascend the track up the opposite valley side and go through another gate. Going straight over an offset fingerpost crossroads (Wp.17 177M), we follow the left fence line and hedge to go over another fingerpost crossroads in a small copse, keeping ahead to emerge at a T-junction (Wp.18 183M). Turning right on a downhill track, we soon enjoy fine views across the **Arun Valley** to **Arundel**, as a track joins from our right. As a hedge and fence line climbs up to us from the right, we turn right by a marker post onto a footpath descending between wire fences (Wp.19 192M) and drop down a very long flight of steps (205!) through light woodland.

Crossing a stile at the bottom, we turn half right to go through a rusty field gate (Wp.20 198M), bearing left on a woodland bridleway before emerging along the base of a curving hanging wood at the edge of the flood plain, rich in wildlife, and the haunt of buzzards. Passing through a field gate, we cross a field to go through another gate, and in 60 yards turn left over a stile at the wood edge (Wp.21 210M), following a surprisingly adventurous, raised footpath, threading through swampy woodland.

Keeping right at a fingerpost junction (Wp.22 219M), we meander on, eventually going under a low railway bridge. We soon cross a footbridge, keeping ahead to the top of a bank and turning right (Wp.23 230M).

We head upstream along the raised riverbank, crossing a stile and keeping along the bank. After crossing a stile we turn left to cross the river over a bridge into the hamlet of **South Stoke**. We pass the church entrance onto a road, then go past cottages to bear right to a fingerpost by three steel field gates (Wp.24 241M).

South Stoke seen from the river bank

For short walk (b) keep ahead at Wp.24, immediately turning right to pass the Victorian brick barn before turning left and following fingerposts to re-join the route, keeping ahead at the kissing gate in the flint wall at Wp.8.

Our way is through the middle gate and down a hedge-lined bridleway, bearing right onto the flood plain at the bottom. Crossing a stile, we follow the right hedge line then, by a marker post, follow the left, water filled ditch. Skirting round a jutting ditch extension, we soon cross a stile by a gate, eventually passing around a lone cottage and heading uphill to emerge through a gate onto a road (Wp.25 258M).

We turn left and, in 60 yards, turn right on a road which rises before descending a deep cutting to return to **The Black Rabbit** (Wp.1 263M), open all day for food and drinks, it can get busy at weekends with its attractive waterside setting.

With no significant climbs, this walk links **Pulborough**, **Amberley** and **Arundel** stations, following the **River Arun** downstream and passing a selection of refreshment opportunities, from fried breakfast at **Pulborough** to dinner in **Arundel**. Our route takes us through contrasting flora, over a medieval bridge, along a disused railway and canal, across a nature reserve, through a Saxon fort, and along the banks of the **River Arun**.

Short Walks	Access:
(a) **Pulborough** station to **Amberley** station (7 miles/11.3km, 2½ hours)	**By train** - check train times on: www.southernrailway.com
(b) **Amberley** station to **Arundel** station, commence walk by turning left from the station, towards **Houghton Bridge** (Wp.14). (5½ miles/8.9km, 2 hours)	**By car** - pay and display parking at **Pulborough** station.

Exiting from the booking hall (Wp.1 0M), we turn left (or right to **The Station Café** for breakfast!), and in 25 yards bear right onto a rising public footpath paralleling the railway. Turning left at a road, we cross over the railway, following the road and turning left at a footpath fingerpost, next to a field gate, as the road bears right (Wp.2 7M). Our path gently climbs, passing a pill box where we bear left before turning right by a marker post, then crossing a T-junction up a rising driveway as we join the **Wey South Path**, following this to **Amberley**. At the top of the drive, passing round a gate, we turn left by a fingerpost (Wp.3 14M), along a lovely woodland path with contrasting flora, so sandy in places that we could be on a beach! At a T-junction by a marker post, we keep left, down the ridge to a road (Wp.4 25M).

Crossing and turning right along the verge over the new bridge, we have a fine view of the Medieval **Stopham Bridge** (re-built 1403), one of England's finest examples. We turn left, back on ourselves, to cross the old bridge, passing **The White Hart Inn**. Keeping right up a short cul-de-sac, we bear right, crossing a stile by a fingerpost onto a grass footpath which takes us over the attractive **River Arun** on a substantial footbridge.

Stopham Medieval Bridge

We cross a field, pass an isolated marker post, and bear slightly left to cross a stile in the hedge line, which, rather disturbingly, has a sign 'Warning Bull in Field' as we LEAVE the meadow! Up a bank ,we cross a concrete river bridge, bearing right up a tarmac road, passing a noisy pumping station and turning right up a concrete access road at a fingerpost T-junction (Wp.5 40M). Turning left in front of a large building on a track between fences, we keep ahead crossing several tracks to the next fingerpost, turning right on a wide track. We briefly join the old railway line to **Petworth** then turn left through a fingerpost field gate. Crossing meadows either side of a rural railway bridge, we emerge over a stile to a busy road. Here we have the option to turn left to visit **Hardham Church** (a 700 yard diversion), with the most complete set of Medieval wall paintings in Britain dated 1130 AD. Crossing the road, we turn right, along the verge, and in 30 yards turn left over a stile (Wp.6 49M).

Passing over a small meadow, we cross a high stile onto a wooded path, dropping to the flood plain and straightening to run along the overgrown **Hardham Canal** towpath, out of use for 90 years, once part of the Arun Navigation linking Surrey to the coast at **Littlehampton**.

The distant Downs from the riverbank below Greatham Bridge

The path, with glimpses of wildfowl in shallow ponds to our left, eventually takes us over a stile to a road (Wp.7 65M), where we turn left. Crossing the 16th century **Greatham Bridge** over the **Arun**, we turn right over a stile onto the raised riverbank, going downstream as we edge nearer to the gap in the Downs.

Crossing a stile, our path takes us away from the river, turning right along a stone surfaced track by a fingerpost (Wp.8 76M), and passing a cottage. Keeping left on the main track, we pass several barns before continuing between fences and turning right on a track at a T-junction by a fingerpost (Wp.9 85M).

Passing a converted barn, we go through a field gate, dropping down to turn left along a meadow edge, go through another gate, and turn right.

The footbridge into Amberley Wild Brooks

As we make for the footbridge (Wp.10 93M), with a sign 'Caution Dangerous Marsh', we enter **Amberley Wild Brooks**, a place of extreme nature, a Site of Special Scientific Interest and of international importance for birds, plants, insects and animals. Fingerposts guide us over stiles, bridges and through gates along the wetland path (impassable during winter floods).

As the path becomes a farm track we keep ahead to eventually climb a slope into the picturesque village of **Amberley** (Wp.11 118M), keeping left on a road into the village.

Turning right at **The Black Horse Inn**, we take the next road on the right, turning left on a footpath by a fingerpost opposite a road junction. Passing between walls and fences, we emerge at a busy road (Wp.12 126M), turn right along the footway and right again immediately after **Amberley Castle** access road, down the concrete **SDW**. Crossing a railway bridge, the track takes us to the raised riverbank, where we turn left, soon crossing a stile. Our path passes behind holiday homes and through a field with an amazing display of teasels, to rejoin the road (Wp.13 145M).

For short walk (a) turn left to follow the signs to **Amberley** station.

We turn right, initially along the footway, passing **The Bridge Inn** and a tearoom, keeping carefully ahead up the narrow **Houghton Bridge**, and turning left to cross the road onto a footpath before crossing the bridge proper (Wp.14 148M). Crossing a stile and a bridge, we turn right over another stile to gain the attractive raised east riverbank, as we continue downstream, passing through the gap in the Downs. We cross a stile and in 45 yards turn left by a fingerpost (Wp.15 156M), crossing another stile to follow the raised, shady footpath across the flood plain.

Passing through a gate, we turn right up a road to a T-junction at **North Stoke** (turn right to visit the church), turning left and immediately right up a footpath by a fingerpost (Wp.16 166M). Crossing two stiles and a meadow, we climb a stile onto a raised footpath through unusual swampy woodland, crossing a very impressive footbridge, eventually emerging over a stile as we return up to the riverbank, turning left to continue downstream. Crossing two stiles by **South Stoke Bridge** (Wp.17 179M), the riverbank path takes us over two more stiles, before we carefully cross stiles either side of the railway line. A grassy track takes us over a stile, as we bear right by a ruin to cross another stile, and along an atmospherically beautiful narrow meadow.

Our path rises, crossing a stile to a fingerpost where we turn left (Wp.18 207M), up a track into the village of **Burpham**. Turning right by the fine church, passing in front of **The George and Dragon Inn**, we go between the high banks of the entrance to the Saxon fort (see Walk 27). Keeping ahead, we pass in front of the village hall, following the left fence line and passing a children's playground to go through a footpath gate leading us to **Jacob's Ladder**, a flight of steps. Descending, we leave the fort to return to the flood plain, crossing a stile and keeping ahead along an embankment. We cross a single, then a double stile, and at the next double stile cross the first (Wp.19 226M), turning sharp left down the bank to cross another stile, keeping ahead onto a grass farm track following a left ditch line. Over a stile by a fingerpost, we turn sharp right to cross a bridge before bearing left, then cross a stile at the edge of a line of poplars. Following the left fence line, we pass through a kissing gate onto a woodland path, emerging at an access road (Wp.20 240M), where we turn right to carefully cross the railway line through kissing gates. Turning left, we cross a stile to regain the raised riverbank which takes us to **Arundel**, with fine views of the town, cathedral and castle as we approach.

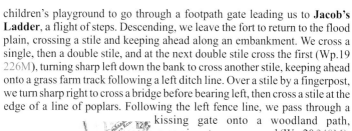

Arundel, from the riverbank

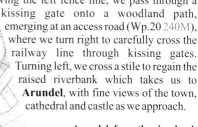

Our path turns left, away from the river, to pass between cottages to a road (Wp.21 261M), where we can turn right to visit **Arundel**, with a wide choice of inns, tearooms and antique emporiums, or left to the station (800 yards) (Wp.22 270M).

A visit to the Romans - **Bignor** has a fine Roman Villa with remarkable mosaic floors. The site, covering over 4 acres, is well worth a visit. But our main interest is **Stane Street**, a Roman Road built in 70 AD which ran from London (Londinium) to Chichester (Noviomagus), virtually in a straight line.

From **Bignor Hill** we descend through woodland to the village and follow a stream through a leafy glade before climbing back up to the top on a wonderful yew-lined terraced track. We wend our way through woodlands, passing **Gumber Farm** and marching up **Stane Street** for a mile and a half to return.

3	2H 55M	7.9 miles/12.7km	⛰	320m / 320m	↻	🍴 0

Access by car:
From the A29 at **Bury**, we follow the signs for **Bignor**. Soon after passing the Roman Villa entrance, keep ahead as the road bends sharp right and in 25 yards, turn left passing a thatched barn. We follow the narrow road for 1.3 miles to the car park at the top of **Bignor Hill**.

Short Walks
(a) For **Bignor**, the leafy stream, and the fine terraced path we follow the route to Wp.9, turning right for the short walk back to the car park(1hour 40 mins, 4.5 miles / 7.2km).

(b) For the Roman Road, we head south from the car park, following the left fence line down a field edge and turning right at the crossroads to join the route from Wp.9 (1hour 15 mins 3.7 miles / 6km).

Extended Walk
For a 15.4 mile/24.8km figure of eight walk, Wp.3 of this walk links with Wp.15 of walk 32.

From the car park (Wp.1 0M) we walk back down the road to turn left at a fingerpost (Wp.2 6M). We drop down a steep slope winding through neglected coppicing onto what appears to be a terraced path, before joining a track by a fingerpost. In 15 yards we turn left down the wood edge, crossing a stile and soon following a spring-fed stream. At the field corner we cross a stile, dropping down to turn right and share our path with the stream.

Crossing a plank bridge, we emerge at a road (Wp.3 27M), turning right to follow the road through **Bignor** to a T-junction, keeping ahead towards the Roman Villa entrance.

At a partly obscured fingerpost (Wp.4 32M), 80 yards before a white cottage, we turn half right, passing a stunted marker post, on a diagonal path across a large field, then follow the right hedge line.

The leafy glade

Crossing a plank bridge, we turn right to cross a footbridge and turn left along a field edge. At a fingerpost (Wp.5 42M), we bear left into an attractive streamside leafy glade, carpeted with the delicate white flower of ramsons in May, with their garlic aroma.

Crossing a plank bridge, then another very bouncy one, we emerge onto a tarmac drive, turning right by a clematis-hidden fingerpost (Wp.6 46M) between a fine timbered cottage and a stone cottage.

We follow the track, keeping left at a fork, to climb a sunken bridleway through the woods onto a stunning, yew tree lined, terraced track. At an offset crossroads (Wp.7 62M), we cross the **SDW**, keeping ahead onto a grass track to the left of a steel gate, following the right fence line.

The turning at Wp.6

We go through a bridleway gate, the path soon opening out onto a fine, rising terraced track. Passing through what may be a temporary makeshift gate, we follow a grass track up a field to go through a bridleway gate, keeping ahead on a farm track.

At the end of the left fence line we bear half right down a large arable field to enter **Barkhale Wood**, soon forking left, uphill, on a flint track. We turn right at a T-junction with **Monarch's Way** (Wp.8 82M). Keeping right at a fork, we follow the track along the edge of a field and cross a farm track. Passing the faint remains of Neolithic camp earthworks in a meadow to our right, we come to a crossroads (Wp.9 95M).

N.B. For short walk (a) turn right to return to **Bignor Hill**. **For short walk (b)**, turn right at Wp.9 to join the route.

We keep ahead on the main track along the wood edge, following the left fence line, with distant views to the coast. At a T-junction (Wp.10 102M), we turn left, and then turn right at the next T-junction. Our route winds through a beech wood on the main track, then along a field edge, following the right fence line.

Gumber Farm flint cottages

After passing through some sparse woodland, we emerge into a field through a bridleway gate (Wp.11 117M), turning right to pass in front of **Gumber Farm** flint cottages before turning left on a track, away from the farm.

Passing through a gate at a wood edge, we turn right in 15 yards onto a woodland path (Wp.12 121M), keeping right at a junction to continue through the narrow wood. At a 6-way junction by an oversize fingerpost (Wp.13 135M), we turn hard right, signed 'Bignor', to climb steadily in the footsteps of the Legions up the Roman road of **Stane Street**. We make our way along the top of the road embankment, still basically sound after nearly 2000 years. As we near the highest point we can look back to see the spire of **Chichester Cathedral** in line with the straight road.

The Roman Road approaching Wp.14

Eventually, after one and a half miles, we climb a stile from the embankment (Wp.14 165M), keeping ahead over the crossroads. At the next crossroads we keep ahead up a narrow grass path to walk along the raised Roman road paralleling the nearby track on our left, with very fine views opening to the south.

At a junction with a wide flint track (Wp.15 171M), we turn right, away from the Roman road, to return to the start (Wp.1 175M).

Our route takes us through every type of woodland - the amazingly beautiful sunlight-dappled wooded footpaths of **Dale Park**, and the mixed forest of **Rewell Wood**, with a surprising amount of ups and downs along the way. With bluebells in spring, wild flowers in summer, autumn leaves and the stark beauty of winter; this is a walk for all seasons.

Slindon is an unspoilt, mainly flint built, estate village, now mostly owned by the National Trust. After threading our way through **Dale Park** we pass the village of **Madehurst** to follow the original winding woodland footpath, walked by past generations of villagers to **Arundel**, once the market town. After an interlude of open fields across the south slopes of the Downs, we return through **Rewell Woods** to **The Newburgh Arms**.

Short Walk

A stunning walk through **Dale Park**. At Wp.7 turn right down a long, extremely wide, tree lined avenue. Bearing right at a copse, cross two stiles and go ahead across an arable field on an obvious farm track. At a fingerpost, turn left and in 50 yards turn right, to walk along the edge of a field next to a wood. Crossing a stile, turn left onto an estate road by a magnificent solitary cypress tree. Just before reaching the gatehouse, turn half right to a fingerpost, to follow the footpath uphill, through the wood, forking right to cross over a bridleway, eventually arriving back at Wp.2, and retracing our steps back to **The Newburgh Arms** (4.3 miles/6.9km).

Access by car:
From the A29, follow the sign for **Slindon**, keeping ahead for ½ mile for roadside parking just south of the pub, **The Newburgh Arms**.

Facing **The Newburgh Arms** (Wp.1 0M), we pass down the left side of the pub, going through gates either side of an old fashioned play park. Almost immediately we turn left, up a tree-lined farm track, turning right at a T-junction onto a road. As we reach a wood we turn left by a fingerpost (Wp.2 6M), keeping on the left footpath to start a wonderful section through the trees of **Dale Park**.

The field edge by Wp.3

Going over a footpath crossroads, downhill, and ignoring a path forking right, we wind through the root systems of some fallen trees to drop down to a wire fence by an enclosed field (Wp.3 22M). Turning left, we follow the fence along the field edge and re-enter the wood, soon bearing right at a T-junction with a footpath (Wp.4 26M).

We follow the clearly defined footpath to another T-junction where we turn left. This straightish stretch takes us through the woods; the local gamekeeper is always 'on the ball', so no poaching! We cross a stile by a gate (Wp.5 38M), turning half right into a field, ultimately aiming for a stile next to a gate in the distant top left corner. Crossing the stile, we turn left onto an uphill flint track (Wp.6 41M) to a junction with an estate road where we keep ahead on the downhill tarmac road. Turning right at a T-junction, with our ears assailed by barking dogs from the nearby kennel, we continue downhill to **New Barn Farm** crossroads (Wp.7 54M).

N.B. For the short walk, turn right here to follow the directions above.

We keep ahead up the hill to a T-junction with a road, where we turn right. At the top of the slope, as the road bends right (Wp.8 60M), we have the option to turn right to visit the pretty **Madehurst Church**. Unfortunately, it always seems to be locked!

However, our path is straight ahead on a track, passing several cottages, to cross a stile by a steel field gate onto the footpath once used as the route to the market town of **Arundel**. Following the hedge line down a field, we cross a double stile, then another at the valley bottom, climbing up to emerge at a road (Wp.9 70M).

Crossing straight over to a fingerpost at the edge of the wood, we follow an uphill path between several large beech trees to a steep climb up a flight of 70 steps, before eventually passing a wooden field gate (Wp.10 80M). We keep ahead to a T-junction with a forestry track, turning left and soon half right down the edge of a pine plantation.

... between large beech trees ...

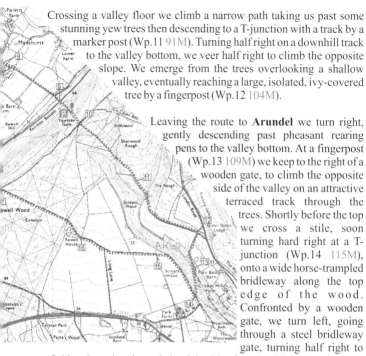

Crossing a valley floor we climb a narrow path taking us past some stunning yew trees then descending to a T-junction with a track by a marker post (Wp.11 91M). Turning half right on a downhill track to the valley bottom, we veer half right to climb the opposite slope. We emerge from the trees overlooking a shallow valley, eventually reaching a large, isolated, ivy-covered tree by a fingerpost (Wp.12 104M).

Leaving the route to **Arundel** we turn right, gently descending past pheasant rearing pens to the valley bottom. At a fingerpost (Wp.13 109M) we keep to the right of a wooden gate, to climb the opposite side of the valley on an attractive terraced track through the trees. Shortly before the top we cross a stile, soon turning hard right at a T-junction (Wp.14 115M), onto a wide horse-trampled bridleway along the top edge of the wood. Confronted by a wooden gate, we turn left, going through a steel bridleway gate, turning half right to cross a field and passing through the right side of a pair of field gates (Wp.15 124M).

We keep ahead on the bridleway between fields with views across the coastal plain to the sea. Arriving at the edge of a wood by a fingerpost (Wp.16 135M), we turn half right into **Rewell Wood**. Our path winds its way onto a straight forest track.

Keeping ahead, we ignore all crossing paths and tracks, until our progress is halted at a bridleway marker post (Wp.17 150M). We pass to the left, soon bearing left to follow the track along an old forest boundary marked by a raised bank and mature trees. In the woods to our left we glimpse the humps and ridges of earthworks of ancient enclosures, evidence that this was once open downland.

The track by the forest boundary

Passing a wooden barrier gate we drop down steeply to a crossroads by a fingerpost (Wp.18 165M), and turn right on a descending track. At the entrance to a scout camp (Wp.19 177M), we turn left, uphill, to cross a nearby stile. After crossing two small meadows and three more stiles we emerge onto a road (Wp.20 182M). Crossing to climb some steps opposite, we follow the footpath to re-join the outward route at the children's playground, returning on to **The Newburgh Arms** (Wp.1 190M).

On this exceptional walk, water is a special feature; we encounter a waterfall, a number of chalk streams, two mill ponds, and cross a real ford.

From **The Cricketers** pub at **Duncton** we pass through **Burton Park**, visiting the tiny but fascinating church before ascending the Downs through the beautiful woods of **Barlavington Hanger**. The equally attractive descent takes us past the delightful **Glatting Farm** then follows shady streams on to **The White Horse Inn** at **Sutton**. We visit **Barlavington Church** in its lovely rural setting and return through woods and fields to **Duncton**.

3 | 2H 50M | 7½ miles/12km | 300m 300m | 2

Access by car: Duncton is on the A285 between **Chichester** and **Petworth**. Roadside parking outside **The Cricketers** pub.

Short Walks

(a) Through **Burton Park** returning past **Duncton Mill**, a pleasant, easy walk. Follow the route to Wp.5 turning right to pick up the route towards Wp.20. (1hour, 2.4 miles/3.9km).

Extended Walk

For a 15.4 mile/24.8km figure of eight route, link Wp.15 of this walk with Wp.3 of Walk 30.

(b) Alternative road parking by **The White Horse Inn**, **Sutton**. A perfect short walk. Start from Wp.16, cross the road at Wp.6 to a steel bridleway gate, and follow the route back to **Sutton**. (1¼ hours, 5 miles/8km).

Facing the inn (Wp.1 0M), we turn left along the verge, turning right just after a bus lay-by through the imposing gates at the entrance to **Burton Park** (Wp.2 2M). Following the estate road winding through woodland, we turn left at a wrought iron gate by a marker post (Wp.3 7M) to cross a plank bridge and stile onto a grass path between fences, the noble façade of **Burton House** visible.

Burton Church

We cross a stile, keeping ahead to visit **Burton Church**. Built in 1075 and much altered over the centuries, it's one of the smallest churches in Sussex but is packed with interesting features; a 15th century screen, one of the oldest fonts in Sussex, three 15th to 16th century tombs, and 16th and 17th century wall paintings.

Leaving the church, we bear left along a tarmac estate road towards the Downs. As the road bends right we keep ahead by a marker post (Wp.4 19M), descending a grass path to pass through an iron gate by a pond and waterfall. Following the left fence line across a field, then uphill along a wood edge, we turn left onto a track at a T-junction (Wp.5 31M).

For short walk (a) turn right at Wp.5 towards Wp.20 above **Duncton Mill**.

Passing to the left of a steel field gate just before a fingerpost (Wp.6 34M), we cross the road, climb up a short slope and go through a bridleway gate.

... wonderful views east ...

We follow the right fence line uphill to enter the stunning woods of **Barlavington Hanger**. At a marker post we fork left (Wp.7 41M), keeping ahead uphill through the trees and eventually emerging onto a path running along the top edge of the woods. Our route runs between hedges before suddenly opening out (Wp.8 55M) with wonderful views to the east along the Downs as far as **Devil's Dyke**.

We drop steeply down **Barlavington Down**, then start to climb the flanks of **Farm Hill**, crossing over a crossroads (Wp.9 62M) and up a wide farm track between arable fields. At the top of the slope we pass through a bridleway gate to meander down through light woodland and scrub on a generously wide track. Leaving a stand of impressive beech trees through a bridleway gate, we keep between sparse and scraggy trees and hedges.

The ancient sunken bridleway

At the top of a rise, the track drops down to a fingerpost (Wp.10 81M) where we turn hard left, down an ancient sunken bridleway, noting the deer runs frequently crossing the track. We turn right by a fingerpost 25 yards after passing two trees on the right with roots growing across the track (Wp.11 88M).

We descend a fine steep footpath, soon traversing left to emerge by a marker post. We cross an arable field and a stream at the bottom of a shallow valley, bearing left across another arable field towards **Glatting Farm**. The medieval village of **Glatting** was abandoned at the time of the Black Death.

Glatting Farm

At a road we turn left (Wp.12 97M), following it as it curves around the attractive farm buildings, then keep

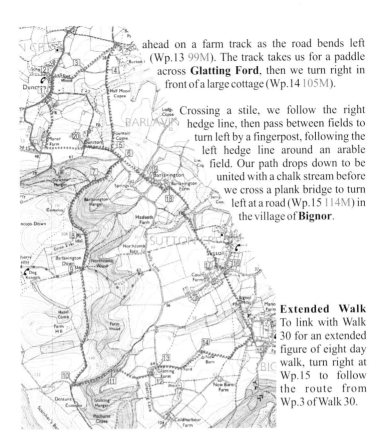

ahead on a farm track as the road bends left (Wp.13 99M). The track takes us for a paddle across **Glatting Ford**, then we turn right in front of a large cottage (Wp.14 105M).

Crossing a stile, we follow the right hedge line, then pass between fields to turn left by a fingerpost, following the left hedge line around an arable field. Our path drops down to be united with a chalk stream before we cross a plank bridge to turn left at a road (Wp.15 114M) in the village of **Bignor**.

Extended Walk
To link with Walk 30 for an extended figure of eight day walk, turn right at Wp.15 to follow the route from Wp.3 of Walk 30.

Passing a row of cottages, we turn left through a garden gate immediately before the next house to descend a grass path that follows a stream through a leafy valley.

We cross two plank bridges, passing **Bignor Mill** upper pond before crossing a sleeper bridge and stile into a field. Our path takes us up to cross a stile on the skyline, turning right and immediately left on a path over an arable field. We pass left of a thatched cottage, then go between fences to drop steeply down to the road opposite **The White Horse Inn** at **Sutton** (Wp.16 125M). (The starting point for **Short Walk (b)**.)

We cross the road, passing in front of the inn, turning left into the car park, up the ramped footpath on the right side, and go through a gate. Turning right through another gate, then turn left up three steps, then right alongside a stone wall to go into what appears to be a back garden. Emerging through a kissing gate (Wp.17 128M), we turn half left diagonally across an arable field to follow a right hedge line, dropping down to an attractive wooded stream.

Crossing a tiny stone bridge (beware of the tiny troll!) and a stile, we keep ahead for 30 yards bearing right to cross an unusual stile in the nearby hedge. Turning left, we follow the left hedge and fence line to a triple apex barn (Wp.18 141M).

We then turn left around a barn and left again, just before a small open-sided barn to enter **Barlavington** churchyard in its picturesque rural setting. Passing through, we keep ahead down a tarmac road, bearing right in 80 yards by a fingerpost up a driveway (Wp.19 144M).

Barlavington Church

Keeping left, we go through a footpath gate, passing an ancient yew tree before dropping down to cross a plank bridge, a road, then climbing steps to cross a stile. Following the right hedge line, we cross a stile between fields and continue to cross another stile, emerging on a road to return to Wp.6 (150M).

For short walk (b) cross the road to go up and through a bridleway gate towards Wp.7.

Turning right onto a track, we retrace our steps to Wp.5, keeping ahead to drop down through woodland to a road above the attractive **Duncton Mill** (Wp.20 155M). We turn left, then right in 45 yards to cross a stile, passing above the top of the mill's feeder stream and keeping ahead across a large field, with **Lavington House** visible in the distance. Heading right by a marker post, we pass behind a large flint wall, then follow the left hedge and fence line downhill.

Crossing a stile, we initially follow the right fence line, continuing ahead on a grass path to enter a wood over a stile. We descend, going over a long, wobbly footbridge across a wide, babbling chalk stream before crossing a stile to emerge onto the road by **The Cricketer's** (Wp.1 168M).

From the attractive village of **East Dean**, we cross the wooded slopes of the Downs of **Goodwood Park** and **Halnaker Park**, with fine views to the sea appearing unexpectedly. We return down the stunning woodland paths of **Bubholts** and back to **The Star and Garter Inn**.

Access by car: Follow the signs for 'East Dean' from the A286 at **Singleton**, or from the A285 via **Droke**. There's roadside parking in the vicinity of **The Star and Garter Inn**.

East Dean village pond

Facing **The Star and Garter** (Wp.1 0M), we turn right towards the village green and pond, turning left, uphill, on the road signposted 'Goodwood/Chichester', soon passing **Manor Farm House**. After a turn half right onto a track by a fingerpost (Wp.2 6M), we soon cross a stile into a field and follow the right fence line to go over a stile in the corner.

Turning half left, we head for woods at the top of **Park Hill**, entering them through a steel field gate. Soon we're going up a narrow, tree-surrounded meadow which doglegs left to take us over a stile at the top end (Wp.3 20M), onto a woodland track.

After crossing a stile by a steel gate, we cross a road (Wp.4 32M), bearing half left along the edge of a countryside car park of the **Goodwood Estate**. We keep to the right, passing through a scattered clump of trees to pick up a faint path along the edge of the main forest. As we reach the far right corner, by a marker post tucked just inside the trees (Wp.5 37M), we ignore a path descending on our right to keep ahead on a leaf-strewn path between regimented lines of beech trees. Emerging through a gate, we turn half right across a field, with distant views to the spire of **Chichester Cathedral** to the right.

Going through gates either side of a diagonal road crossing (Wp.6 47M), we turn right along a field edge, paralleling the road, enjoying sea views over **Bognor** (no sniggering, it really is a nice place), and **Halnaker** windmill on the skyline to our left. At the corner of the large field we turn left onto a track which soon veers right through woodland. Emerging from the trees, our track bears left downhill, passing some beehives amongst yew trees; then, as the track straightens out to drop downhill, we fork left by a partially hidden fingerpost (Wp.7 61M) on a footpath down through the trees. At a T-junction we turn left on a long, straight, rising forest ride, keeping ahead over the first crossroads. As the track opens out near the top of the slope, we turn left at a crossroads immediately after a marker post hidden on our left (Wp.8 91M). Following the open track, we cross a stile by a steel barrier gate leading onto a road which we cross diagonally to a fingerpost to the left, following a footpath across an arable field and enter a wood.

At a T-junction with a bridleway we turn left and, in 25 yards, fork right (Wp.9 101M) down an attractive woodland footpath. Keeping ahead over an angled crossroads, we keep right at a fork, and go over a stile to cross a small field with lovely views to the surrounding Downs. We re-enter the woods, crossing or going round a stile, and follow a superb terraced path as it winds its way round, just inside the edge of **Bubholts Wood**.

Bubholts Wood

On reaching a T-junction with a bridleway we turn right (Wp.10 116M), descending through a gate and along a field edge, following the left fence line towards **East Dean** below, dropping down to a sunken track and turning left. After passing some charming estate workers' flint cottages, we arrive back at the pub (Wp.1 125M). As a point of interest, the row of flint cottages opposite the pub boast an unusual feature; their corners have been skilfully crafted from flint, as opposed to the usual easier option of brick or stone.

Levin Down is the largest chalk heathland in West Sussex. The nature reserve is home to some of the last remaining juniper trees on the South Downs. **Singleton** is another attractive, mainly flint, estate workers' village - only recently has any modern building taken place here.

We climb across the panoramic slopes of **Hat Hill**, covered in wild flowers in summer, passing the isolated **Downley Cottage** in the heart of the Downs. We return through **Singleton Forest**, across **Levin Down** and back through the village to **The Partridge Inn**.

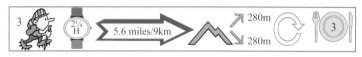

Access by car:
Singleton is on the A286, north of **Chichester**. Turn into the village and park in the lane alongside the pub and garden.

Facing the front of **The Partridge Inn** (Wp.1 0M), we turn left along a narrow street to a T-junction with the main road. After turning left along the footway, we cross the road in 20 yards to go along a driveway, passing to the left of a field gate.

After following the boundary of the cricket pitch, we go behind the pavilion to cross a stile.

Short Walk

This route allows you to enjoy the delights of **Levin Down** and return to the village. Facing **The Partridge Inn**, turn right along the road, eventually turning left at a fingerpost next to the modern village school.

Follow the grass footpath up, crossing a stile near the top of the hill and bearing slightly left up to a fingerpost to turn right onto a grass bridleway across a large meadow. At a lone fingerpost, keep ahead on the bridleway and pass through a field gate. Follow the left fence line until it veers left, and then bear right across the meadow to go through a steel field gate. Keep ahead to a fingerpost on a flint track, and turn right to follow the route from Wp.7. (1 hour 10 mins, 3miles/4.8km)

Following the right fence line, we cross another stile, keeping ahead to soon cross a further stile by a National Trust sign (Wp.2 7M). We go up a gently rising 'tree tunnel' track, passing over the old railway line to climb a flight of steps and cross a stile at the top. Up the slopes of the organic meadow of **Hat Hill**, a profusion of wild flowers in summer, we keep left to pass under power lines and eventually cross a stile in the top left corner.

Keeping ahead up the left edge of an arable field, we pass through a 'contraption of gates' and up the next edge of a large field. A sleeper stile takes us across its corner, where we turn right along the next two field edges before dropping down to turn right at a T-junction with a track. In 15 yards we fork left on a descending track (Wp.3 37M), keeping ahead to pass round the remote **Downley Cottage** (see photo on the next page).

Continuing between hedges to a marker post, we turn left to follow the right hedge line, to gently descend a tranquil valley. We pass to the right of a barn as we flit in and out of a wood before continuing down a field edge. Our track curves away from a wood, passing between fields and descending to eventually emerge at a busy road at **Littlewood Farm** (Wp.4 57M) where we go left along the verge, crossing the road to turn right at the next turning, up the access road to **Singleton Oilfield**.

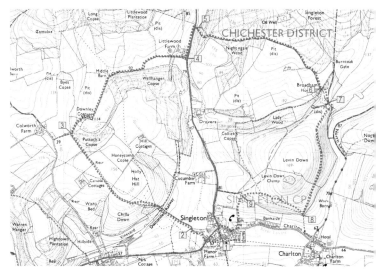

In 40 yards we bear left onto a bridleway (Wp.5 63M), climbing up through a wood. (Yes, there is oil under the Downs here, around 6 million barrels apparently!)

Foxgloves, Singleton Forest

Emerging onto the road, we turn left, and in 35 yards turn right by a fingerpost on a woodland track, climbing to keep ahead at a T-junction. We descend through dense coppicing, briefly emerging at a valley bottom, before continuing up the opposite side.

We follow a delightful winding bridleway just inside the edge of **Singleton Forest**, with some fine trees along the edge and amazing displays of foxgloves in patches of cleared woodland in June and July.

Soon after a farm track joins from our right we leave the forest, dropping down to a fingerpost crossroads (Wp.6 87M) by **Broadham House**. Continuing ahead, we climb the sunken track to the left, which soon curves right to follow the left fence line. As our route joins a track we turn left between posts, to a 4-way fingerpost in the bushes to our left (Wp.7 91M). Keeping ahead, we go downhill on the flint track, turning right in 75 yards up a steep bank by a fingerpost, then crossing a stile into a meadow. We follow the left fence line to cross a stile on our left, onto a delightfully winding woodland path, that traverses the hillside.

Over a stile, we enter the **Sussex Wildlife Trust Nature Reserve**, following a meandering path along the flanks of **Levin Down** with great views of the adjacent Downs and village of **Charlton**. After passing through two footpath gates, we descend to an information board (Wp.8 112M) by a gate where we turn hard right on a rising path that soon takes us through a scattering of junipers before crossing a stile at a fence corner.

Threading our way ahead through more junipers and scrub, we eventually cross a double stile and maintain direction on a faint grass path across the lower slopes of an organic meadow. Descending gently, we cross the stile that's visible in the hedge line below (Wp.9 112M).

An obvious wide path takes us down to pass an amazing tree and a school, before we turn right onto a road, keeping right on a road through the attractive village. We turn left at the pond, passing the village pump on our return to **The Partridge Inn** (Wp.1 134M).

The nearby **Weald and Downland Open Air Museum** is excellent, and well worth a visit.

The Partridge Inn, Singleton

A challenging scarp slope adventure, on steep, narrow and twisting footpaths. We start from **The Unicorn Inn** at **Heyshott**, crossing farmland before climbing the wooded scarp slope. Between two short, sedate stretches of the South Downs way, we visit eight Bronze Age barrows before dropping into the stunning **Heyshott Escarpment Nature Reserve** and crossing high above the abandoned, now grassy, 1930s pit workings. We climb back to the top before descending down a beautiful woodland footpath, to return through the straggling village.

Access by car:
From the A286 between **Chichester** and **Midhurst** take the turning for **Heyshott** 1½ miles south of **Midhurst**, turning right at **Heyshott Green** and parking outside **The Unicorn Inn**.

Manor Farm yard

Facing **The Unicorn Inn**, we turn left (Wp.1 0M), through the village. As the road bends sharply to the left, we keep ahead up the driveway to **Manor Farm**, soon taking the right fork. We pass through the farmyard startled by a kennel of gun dogs, as we make for a farm track between hedges.

Turning right onto a bridleway track at the second T-junction, by a marker post (Wp.2 15M), we head towards the Downs. Going through a gate, our track bends left in a cutting. We keep ahead at a fork, along a wood edge, passing through a gate, and emerging at a fingerpost where we keep ahead across a field to go through a gate. We cross another field to a crossroads by a marker post (Wp.3 31M), turning right to follow the left hedge line.

Entering the wooded scarp slope across a tree trunk stile, we divert round some fallen trees before turning left on a woodland track. Our track undulates inside the wood edge, offering pleasing glimpses across the fields. At a fork by a marker post we keep left, turning hard right at a T-junction with a track, then immediately left up a very steep bank by a marker post (Wp.4 50M). We climb a delightful, winding woodland footpath, crossing a forest track and clambering over fallen trees until we turn right at a T-junction.

At a crossroads, we keep ahead, soon turning right through a field gate into the organic **Long Meadow** (Wp.5 63M), tended by the Graffham Down Trust. Finding our own path through the meadow, we leave through a field gate at the far end, keeping ahead to join with the tree-lined **SDW**. As a meadow appears on our right, we turn right between posts (Wp.6 83M), following the faint grass path over cross dykes to pass eight Bronze Age barrows. We leave the meadow at its south-west end, turning right to rejoin the **SDW**. We keep ahead over the first crossroads, turning right, over a stile, at the next (Wp.7 100M).

... fabulous views over Heyshott ...

Crossing a meadow, we pass a concrete trig point, keeping ahead and dropping down, with fabulous views across **Heyshott** and the Weald. Crossing a stile, we enter the beautiful Nature Reserve, steeply descending a chalky path, soon keeping to the left fork on the main path, before we turn right.

Dropping down to a flattish, grassy area (Wp.8 109M), we turn left, seeking our hard-to-spot path in the bushes; following it, we circle around and above the old pit workings.

The steep terraced bridleway

After crossing two stiles, we climb a flight of steps on a superb winding path, high up the slope to emerge into an open area of humps and bumps, keeping left as we descend; look hard left, up the line of the fence, seeking a stile (Wp.9 121M). Climbing over, we turn left up an attractive, steep, terraced

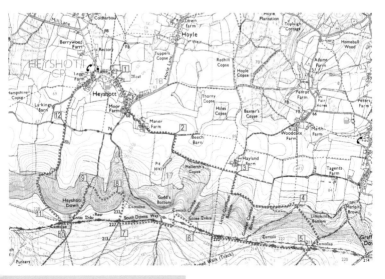

bridleway, emerging at the top to cross a field and go though (or by-pass) a bridleway gate to turn right, briefly joining the **SDW**. We pass between more cross dykes to a nearby 5-way fingerpost junction (Wp.10 133M), turn half right on an invisible path across a field, and aim for the far left edge of the wood ahead.

We're searching for the remains of a stile, which almost reluctantly appears in a gap in the fence at the wood edge by a marker post (Wp.11 137M). Crossing, we follow a fine, steeply winding, woodland footpath down to a T-junction, where we turn left, eventually emerging at an oddly shaped crossroads by a flint barn.

Fine cottages as we enter Heyshott

Continuing ahead on a farm track to a T-junction of farm tracks, we again keep ahead between a post and rail barrier (Wp.12 154M), to cross a field to a road. Turning right, we pass fine cottages and farm buildings as we enter **Heyshott**. Passing a hall on our right, we bear right between stumpy posts on a grass path, soon taking us to join the road opposite the attractive church.

We bear right, along the road, passing the old village smithy on our left, as we return to **The Unicorn Inn** (Wp.1 167M). Like so many, it's more restaurant than pub, but has a great garden for a summer's day.

When testing this walk, we left the car in the pub car park with the blessing of the landlady, having offered reassurance that we would be back for a post-walk pint. Our honesty and integrity were called into question, as we returned to find our car very effectively blocked in by the vehicle of a doubting landlord! Park, but fail to patronize, at your peril!

Kingley Vale National Nature Reserve contains a grove of ancient yews, amongst the oldest living things in Britain, twisted and gnarled like a 'Tolkein' forest. None but the brave come here at dusk - legends of witches and ghosts abound! A favourite haunt of Tennyson, in life - and after death!

From **The Hare and Hounds** pub we head north-west through a patchwork of fields, woods and tranquil valleys, with wonderful views as we drop down to **Walderton**. Passing **The Barley Mow** pub, we climb up to the open Downs to the magical **Kingley Vale**. After a steep climb through a yew forest we visit the **Devil's Humps** - Bronze Age barrows, before returning down the slopes of **Stoughton Down**.

4	3¾ H	9.7 miles/15.6km	470m ↕ 470m	↻	4

Short Walks

(a) A tranquil walk through woods, fields and valleys. Follow the route to Wp.10 keeping ahead on the bridleway to **Stoughton**, turning left at the road to return. (1½ hours, 4.4 miles/7km)

(b) A circular walk taking in **Walderton**, **Kingley Vale** and **Stoughton**. Facing **The Hare and Hounds** turn left towards the village, forking right to pass the church entrance, then up a flinty bridleway. Keeping left at a fork and passing over the brow of the hill, turn left at a marker post at Wp.10 onto a footpath. (2½ hours, 6.6 miles/10.6km)

(c) A great family walk to the amazing 2½km **Kingley Vale Nature Trail** (collect guide from the hut). Alternative parking at **West Stoke** car park, follow the signs from the B2178 north of **Chichester**. (1hour 20 mins, 3.1m/5km)

Access by car:
From the B2146 at **Walderton**, follow the signs for **Stoughton** (roadside parking by **The Hare and Hounds** pub).

Facing the pub (Wp.1 0M), we take the footpath running up the right hand side, crossing stiles either side of a meadow before following a right fence line up to a wood. Turning left by a marker post on a leaf strewn path for 50 yards to another marker post, we turn right to go over a stile (Wp.2 9M). Guided by fingerposts along a rising path, we keep ahead over three forest tracks on a gently deviating path through a stunning beech wood, to emerge over a stile. Maintaining direction, we cross a field to a marker post at the far end of a hedge to the left of **Pitlands Farm**. We turn right to go through the farmyard and up the farm track ahead, along the shoulder of a tranquil valley. Passing a pit within a copse, we drop down to an isolated T-junction fingerpost (Wp.3 23M) to turn left across the field, then follow the track along the edge of a wood. At a fingerpost T-junction (Wp.4 29M), we turn left onto a bridleway track, turning right at a T-junction with a road (Wp.5 35M). After the uphill road bears right, a left turn over a stile by a steel gate takes us onto a snaking woodland track descending to a T-junction (Wp.6 41M), where we turn left. The track descends to run along a field edge, then into an impressive wood to a fingerpost T-junction where we turn right, uphill, taking the next left fork

(Wp.7 49M) on a track curving and climbing to pass a fingerpost. Towards the top of a slope, by a marker post, we fork right, crossing a stile by a cottage with a profusion of snow drops in February, and continue to a fingerpost T-junction (Wp.8 57M). Forking left on a bridleway winding through field and wood, ignoring all crossing tracks, we come to a road (Wp.9 67M). Crossing, we follow the left hedge line up a field and on into light woodland. Climbing towards the top of a slope, by a marker post (Wp.10 72M), we turn right onto a footpath.

For the short walk (a) we keep ahead at Wp.10, following the bridleway down to **Stoughton**, turning left at the road to return to the pub.

Emerging from the wood, we cross a field with glorious views opening out on all sides. Following the obvious path, crossing a road, taking guidance from marker and fingerposts we thread our way to turn left between houses into **Walderton** to a T-junction with a road (Wp.11 86M). Turning right and after passing a fine thatched flint cottage, we turn left descending to cross the winterbourne **River Ems**, soon turning left at a T-junction with a road. We pass **The Barley Mow pub**, and as we leave the village, we turn up a track on the right (Wp.12 93M). By a barrier gate and Forestry Commission sign 'Walderton Down', we bear left to climb a terraced forest track. At the top, by a marker post, we fork right on a narrowing path to turn right before a stile, leaving the wood (Wp.13 108M). Passing a ruined flint barn, we turn left on a rising track between fences along the ridge. The higher we get the better the view behind us becomes. At a triangular T-junction in woodland, we fork left by a marker post (Wp.14 124M), yew trees becoming more frequent as we approach the Reserve. At a field corner by a fingerpost, as the main track veers left, we keep ahead, downhill, into woodland and then along the wood edge, with the spire of **Chichester Cathedral** visible ahead as the path opens out.

At a stile by an information board, we cross into **Kingley Vale Nature Reserve** (Wp.15 138M), turning right down a gently winding attractive footpath, fragrant with wild thyme in summer. We descend through the edge of the Reserve to the main entrance by a kissing gate (Wp.16 148M), turning left to visit the field centre hut, from where we turn right to follow the main track and Nature Trail marker posts. At point 4, by an information board, we turn right into the highlight of the walk, the amazing, eerie, fantasy world of the ancient yew grove.

The ancient yew grove

We follow the trail left at point 5, (for the more adventurous types, keep to the right hand lesser path to scramble your way over and under the snaking limbs of the ancient trees - if you lose your way go back to point 5 and follow the proper route!). We leave the trees, turning right and still following the Nature Trail along the track to enter another incredibly magical yew tree grove, emerging at point 11 (Wp.17 166M).

For walk (c) turn right, following the Nature Trail marker posts.

We keep ahead up the wide, rising grass path, which narrows as we approach the younger yew forest. Threading our way through the trees up the very steep hill (good grips on footwear essential), we keep to the main path, finally emerging and turning left to pass through a kissing gate (Wp.18 180M). As the path opens out, we bear right, uphill, and make for the first bowl barrow of the four **Devil's Humps**.

They consist of two Bronze Age bowl barrows and two bell barrows, the latter being about 500 years later. Legend has it that if you run round all four, six times without stopping (about 2 ½ miles!), the Devil will appear. We turn west to visit the other three; the views are beautiful and far ranging on a clear day.

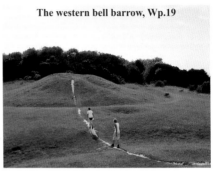

The western bell barrow, Wp.19

From the top of the western bell barrow (Wp.19 190M) we turn half right to a wide, sometimes muddy, track between trees taking us to a T-junction where we turn right (Wp.20 200M).

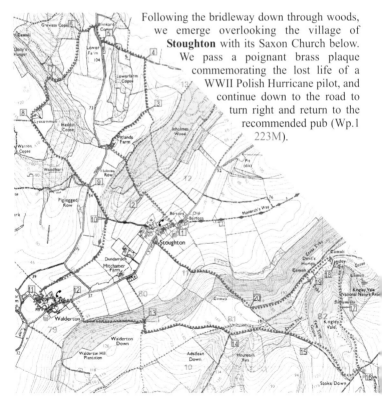

Following the bridleway down through woods, we emerge overlooking the village of **Stoughton** with its Saxon Church below. We pass a poignant brass plaque commemorating the lost life of a WWII Polish Hurricane pilot, and continue down to the road to turn right and return to the recommended pub (Wp.1 223M).

A different landscape to the high Downs, patches of woodland interspersed with fields but still with plenty of satisfying views and a good chance of spotting some deer. We start from the rural village of **East Marden** with its unique thatched well-house, then cross fields and woodland to **The White Horse Inn** at Chilgrove.

East Marden's well-house

We return on attractive paths towards **East Marden** before climbing through a fine bluebell wood to **Up Marden**, to visit the remote and hidden atmospheric church.

3 | 2H 50M | 7½ miles/12.1km | 330m / 330m | ⟳ | 1

Short Walks

(a) A pleasing walk from **East Marden** to **Chilgrove** returning over **Bow Hill**. Follow the route to Wp.9, keeping ahead and turning right at a road to return to the well house (1¾ hours, 4.7 miles/7.7km).

(b) Best in late April to early May for the bluebells and ramsons. On mainly quiet footpaths climbing to **Up Marden Church**, returning down a steep wooded hangar to **East Marden**. From the well-house, take the road signed 'Stoughton', turning left up a concrete farm access to turn right at Wp.9, between barns, following the route to the end (1 hour 10 mins, 3 miles/5.1km)

Access by car:
From the B2141 between **South Harting** and the A286 north of **Chichester**, take the turning signed 'East Marden' between **North Marden** and **Chilgrove**. Limited roadside parking 50 yards from the well house, up the road signed 'North Marden'.

From the unique thatched village well-house (Wp.1 0M), we walk up the road past the church (which has the notable distinction of housing Prince Albert's rather ornate organ), turning left by a footpath fingerpost after the last cottage on the left as we leave the village. Crossing a stile onto a diagonal path, we cross a small field and another stile to follow the left hedge and fence line up a large field. We cross further stiles either side of the wooded track of **Long Lane** to go up an arable field and over another stile, bearing half right to cross a stile by a steel gate (Wp.2 20M). Turning left along the road verge we then turn right, crossing by the 'Hooksway' sign and turn right again in 30 yards over a stile (Wp.3 23M).

We follow the right fence line with striking views over the wooded valley and a good chance of buzzard-spotting. Crossing a stile, we descend a lovely path down the valley side to cross stiles either side of the flat grassy bottom. We enter a wood, immediately turning right along the bridleway of **Philliswood Lane** (Wp.4 30M).

At a T-junction we turn right, downhill, passing under power lines to turn half left across a stile, loosely following the left fence line. We cross a field to climb stiles either side of an access road, crossing another field and going over another stile. We keep ahead, the field funnelling us towards a stile at the end. Going over, we turn left along a roadside verge to a road junction, with **The White Horse Inn** to our left (more restaurant than pub, but by all means give it a try).

Keeping ahead along the left verge of the main road, we soon cross to turn right up a stony uphill wooded track by a bridleway fingerpost (Wp.5 53M). At the top we turn right through a gate (Wp.6 64M) up a ridge across fields passing to the right of a copse, with lovely views across **The Solent** and **The Isle of Wight** opening out as we gently climb. We go through a bridleway and three field gates onto a concrete drive, passing to the left of two cottages at **Bow Hill Farm**. As the drive bears right, we keep left to cross a stile (Wp.7 83M) on a footpath between wire fences, then follow the left fence line through a gate and over a stile to turn right onto a downhill farm track. At a road we turn left, then right at a fingerpost by a barn conversion and small cottage (Wp.8 89M). Descending a footpath through a wood edge, we cross a stile, emerging to cross a field and heading towards a gap in the trees with **East Marden** nestling below.

Dropping steeply down, we cross a stile near the bottom left corner, going through a coppice

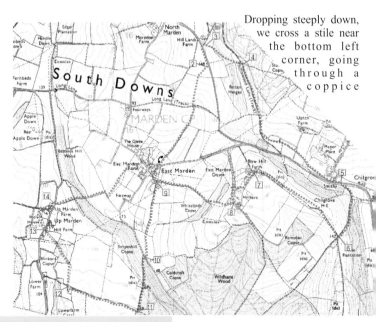

and passing a disused pump house to cross another stile. We follow the right fence line down a field edge, crossing two stiles and turning left immediately after an open barn, between farm buildings (Wp.9 104M).

For short walk (a)
Keep ahead down the concrete road turning right at the bottom to return to the well house.

For short walk (b)
Come up the concrete track to turn right at Wp.9)

Passing through the farmyard, we go over a stile which may be somewhat hidden by undergrowth, following the right fence line down the field edge to another stile. Crossing, we now follow the left fence to cross two more stiles, then go diagonally across a field towards the wooded hillside. Turning left along a road, we immediately cross, turning right up a rising woodland track (Wp.10. 114M), with beech mast crunching under our feet. Emerging at the top, we keep ahead along the wood edge, turning right immediately after a T-junction on our left (Wp.11 123M). We follow the right tree line along field edges with unexpected glimpses of the **Isle of Wight**.

Blinkard Copse

The path becomes a track between trees, leading to a stable block and flint cottage where we turn right by a marker post (Wp.12 132M), then cross a field to enter a wood, bearing half left on the obvious path through **Blinkard Copse**, with its stunning bluebell and wood anemone-covered floor in late April.

We emerge over a stile, diagonally crossing a field to cross three stiles to the left of a dark timber-clad stable block onto a road (Wp.13 142M). Here we turn right, then left in 30 yards over a stile to cross a meadow, passing **Up Marden's** restored well-house, before bearing right into a copse. Hidden inside is **Up Marden Church**, a simple unrestored candlelit 13th century church, with an almost unique atmosphere of ages past. Walking round the church we leave on a gravel path, turning right along a flint track and turning left at a T-junction along a rising road. In 100 yards, just past the entrance to **Up Marden Farm**, we turn right by a fingerpost (Wp.14 152M).

Going down a track, we soon pass to the left of a marker post, following the right hedge line downhill. We plunge down a steeply wooded slope and over a footpath crossroads, crossing the woodland floor, carpeted in ramsons near the bottom, to emerge, following the right fence line down a field edge. Crossing a stile, we turn right, then left, around a field edge, eventually crossing a simple stile onto a diagonal path across a meadow. We cross a final stile in the corner, turning right down the road to return to **East Marden** (Wp.1 170M).

Great views, fascinating history, wonderful church, and a feast of 'off the beaten track' footpaths to enjoy.

We head east over **Harting Downs** and **Beacon Hill**, overlooking the village of **Treyford** before visiting the Bronze Age **Devil's Jumps**. A sudden change of landscape takes us into the peaceful heart of the South Downs, to pass an abandoned medieval village before a beautiful footpath to **The Royal Oak** at **Hooksway**. We return past the delightful church of **North Marden** on fine paths through field and wood.

Access by car:
Take the B2141 between **Lavant** and **South Harting**. Park in the car park near the top of **Harting Hill**, indicated by the brown sign 'Harting Downs', parking at the north-east end.

Very Short Walk
Across **Harting Downs** and descending a pretty valley, returning through wood and meadow. Follow the route to Wp.2, turning right down **Bramshott Bottom** on a footpath. Turn right at a crossroads, following the path steeply up through the woods and taking the next right turn to rejoin our route at Wp.18, at the entrance to the meadow. (1 hour 5 mins, 2.7 miles/4.3km)

Looking over South Harting

From the north-east end of the car park (Wp.1 0M), looking north, we turn right (E), going through a nearby bridleway gate next to a field gate, on the superior path above the **SDW**. As we crest the first summit, we are rewarded with views over **South Harting** and across the **Weald** before descending to go over cross dykes (Iron Age earthworks, thought to have been control points for the movement of people and animals along the ridgeway).

Loosely following the left hedge line, we drop down through a wide gap in the scrub going through a bridleway gate on a descending chalky path. Passing through another gate, we keep ahead to the valley floor (Wp.2 20M), **Bramshott Bottom**.

N.B. For the Short Walk, turn right along the valley bottom, description as above.

We continue ahead, climbing steeply up through a bridleway gate and bearing right to the summit of **Beacon Hill**, an Iron Age hill fort (600-500BC) with wonderful views in all directions.

Looking east from Beacon Hill

Continuing east, we pass a nearby fingerpost as we drop downhill, taking the left fork to pass a cluster of gates at the valley bottom (Wp.3 35M). Our climb up **Pen Hill** follows the right fence line, over cross dykes, then descends to a four-way fingerpost to turn sharp right, signed 'SDW'.

We keep ahead at a fingerpost crossroads, along the top edge of a hanging wood, then follow the left fence line. Still following the **SDW**, we wind our way to a T-junction with a farm track (Wp.4 54M), turning left on a rising stony track before leaving the **SDW** and descending to a tarmac road overlooking the village of **Treyford**. Just before the road bends sharply left, we turn right by a 'hard to spot' fingerpost (Wp.5 62M), up a delightful, steepish, lightly wooded footpath, to eventually cross stiles either side of a track. Crossing a stile, we cross a small meadow before bearing left in a wood, climbing to cross another stile.

To our right, between gaps in the hedge, we glimpse the nearby **Devil's Jumps**, the best example of a Bronze Age cemetery on the South Downs, the alignment orientated to the setting of the sun on midsummer's day. Over a stile (Wp.6 80M), we turn right onto the **SDW**, soon heading right up a short path to go over another stile to visit the **Jumps**; the best view is from the last barrow.

Leaving over the same stile, we turn right to regain the **SDW**, gently descending through woodland, to a crossroads by a fingerpost (Wp.7 94M). After turning left, we soon cross a stile into a contrasting farmland landscape, and pass down the right edge of a meadow. We bear right down a special valley, a rare place where the sounds of modern day living are absent, deep in the mid-Downs. As we pass through a field gate more secrets are revealed.

On our left, are just discernible earth banks, platforms and trackways, the buried remains of the medieval village of **Monkton**, abandoned in the 16th century. As we pass the remains of the fenced-off farmhouse and information board, we cross a stile, continuing to a fingerpost by a flint building (Wp.8 106M). We turn sharp right up the grass slope on an invisible path, (not the track bearing right), to cross a stile in the top right corner.

Our route follows an open aspect footpath along field edges and eventually passes through a kissing gate at a field corner, onto a charming, wide grass path through light woodland.

A fingerpost points us right onto a woodland track for 65 yards, then, using the direction indicated by another fingerpost (Wp.9 118M), we take the footpath dissecting two diverging tracks. The wonderful grass path takes us through juvenile woodland, keeping ahead to eventually drop down through a beech wood to a stile.

The Royal Oak, Hooksway (Wp.10)

Crossing, we bear right then left to visit, or pass, the charming **Royal Oak** at **Hooksway** (Wp.10 128M).

Continuing up the road, we turn hard right onto a 'tree tunnel' bridleway (Wp.11 132M), eventually taking the second opening on our left onto a footpath by a hidden fingerpost (Wp.12 141M), as the track bends sharply right.

The tree-lined path emerges at a road, where we turn right along the verge, soon crossing to take the road signed 'North Marden'. As the road bends left, we turn right through a double gate (Wp.13 149M), on a track, soon keeping to the right fork and to the right of a post and rail fence to visit the very special **North Marden Church**, a 'step back in time'.

North Marden Church

Founded in the 12th century, the candlelit church has a semi-circular end, unique on the Downs, its shape and simplicity a delight.

We leave the church, turning right on a track which soon becomes a path between fences by a fingerpost, then follow the right fence line downhill to cross a stile. Taking the obvious footpath (guided by fingerposts), we go through light woodland.

A fingerpost directs us right, following the left hedge line along arable field edges, then keeping ahead to a footpath junction by a marker post (Wp.14 163M). Continuing ahead, we meander up the middle of a long, thin copse, eventually crossing a stile at a four-way junction (Wp.15 170M), where we turn sharp right along a field edge.

Following the right fence and hedge lines, we cross (or pass) two stiles, occasionally glimpsing a distant **Uppark House** on our left. Keeping ahead at a fingerpost junction, we join a bridleway to pass an imposing, ornate gatehouse of **Uppark**, before staying ahead on a wide track. Turning left immediately before a road, we soon cross the road onto a bridleway opposite (Wp.16 186M). At a marker post we turn left, following the right fence line along a field edge before entering a wood to turn right at a crossroads (Wp.17 191M).

Through a nearby kissing gate, we fork left, then bear left as a path joins us from our right. After passing to the right of a kissing gate into a long, narrow organic meadow (Wp.18 193M), we follow a wide grass path up the meadow's left side, turning right then left, by a gate and stile, onto the grass track up its centre.

Our route climbs to the top of **Harting Downs** and passes to the left of a dew pond, and after bearing half left, downhill, we pass through the bridleway gate to return to the car park (Wp.1 210M).

The Red Lion is claimed as Hampshire's oldest inn, originally used by the craftsmen who built the church opposite in the 12th century. **St Hubert's Chapel** at **Idsworth** is thought to have been built by Earl Godwin, King Harold's dad, and stands in isolated simplicity.

Starting from the village 'square' of **Compton**, we cross undulating downland, passing through forest to **The Red Lion** at **Chalton**. The return follows the **Staunton Way** over **Chalton Down** before we visit the atmospheric **Idsworth Chapel**, with a fascinating mix of meadow and woodland for the last leg.

| 3 | 🚶 | ⌚ 3¼ H | ⬌ 8.8 miles/14.2km | ⛰ | ↗ 310m ↘ 310m | 🔄 | 🍴 3 |

Short Walks

(a) A wide circuit around **Compton Down**. Follow the route from **Compton**, turn left at Wp.4 on the bridleway, over **Cowdown Lane** (track), and cross a road on an offset junction. Continue ahead up a wooded slope on the bridleway, turn left at the fingerpost T-junction at the top of the slope at Wp.12. (5.2 miles/8.4km, 1 hour 50 mins)

(b) The Red Lion and **Idsworth Chapel**. Use alternative roadside parking, by the path to the chapel, on the road between **Buriton** and **Finchdean**. Start from Wp.10 and turn left at the fingerpost T-junction at Wp.12. In 140 yards fork left, downhill, on the bridleway and cross the road on an offset junction. Follow the bridleway over **Cowdown Lane** (track), and climb the ridge to turn left at the marker post T-junction to rejoin the route at Wp.4. (6.8 miles/10.9km, 2 hours 30 mins)

Access by car:
Compton is on the B2146 between **South Harting** and **West Marden**. Park in the village square by **The Coach and Horses**.

From the village 'square' (Wp.1 0M), we walk back to the main road, turning right through the village, taking care as there's no footway in places. After leaving the village, keeping to the left verge where possible, we turn left at a fingerpost (Wp.2 8M), crossing a stile. We loosely follow the left fence line, crossing a stile and turning right, initially on a track, then up a bank, keeping ahead on a vague

path up a wooded meadow to cross a stile by a tree, which appears in the fence ahead. Crossing a road, we pass through a small copse, cross an arable field, and pass through squeezes either side of **Cowdown Lane**. We cross two more arable fields with squeezes, before dropping down to a tarmac lane (Wp.3 25M).

Turning left, we follow the lane, passing **Eckensfield**, keeping ahead on a stony, rising track. At the top of the slope, by a marker post (Wp.4 35M) (**For short walk (a)** turn left here as described above), we keep ahead, now following our panoramic track downhill and along a wood edge. As the track veers left towards a house, we turn right by a fingerpost, back on ourselves, on a descending terraced woodland path. Ten yards after passing a marker post on our left, we take a short cut by turning left and dropping down to emerge on a wide forest track (Wp.5 44M). We turn left, along the **Sussex Border Path**, the forest vibrant with birdsong in spring. Keeping ahead over a fingerpost crossroads, we fork right by a marker post (Wp.6 59M), on a winding woodland path before emerging to follow a left fence line. Passing a house, we cross a road, continuing ahead to go over a railway footbridge.

Looking back from above the organic meadow

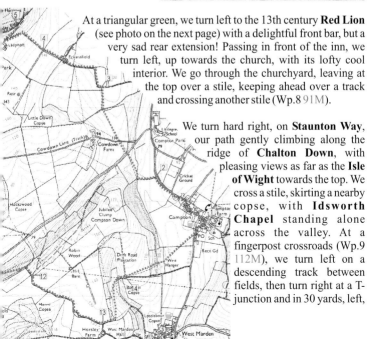

Emerging at a road, we turn left, and in 30 yards turn right (Wp.7 70M), up a footpath. Crossing an awkward stile, we climb a steep organic meadow, soon crossing two more stiles and a large arable field, our route marked by posts. On reaching a road, we turn right, descending into **Chalton** village.

At a triangular green, we turn left to the 13th century **Red Lion** (see photo on the next page) with a delightful front bar, but a very sad rear extension! Passing in front of the inn, we turn left, up towards the church, with its lofty cool interior. We go through the churchyard, leaving at the top over a stile, keeping ahead over a track and crossing another stile (Wp.8 91M).

We turn hard right, on **Staunton Way**, our path gently climbing along the ridge of **Chalton Down**, with pleasing views as far as the **Isle of Wight** towards the top. We cross a stile, skirting a nearby copse, with **Idsworth Chapel** standing alone across the valley. At a fingerpost crossroads (Wp.9 112M), we turn left on a descending track between fields, then turn right at a T-junction and in 30 yards, left,

The Red Lion

descending towards the railway line. A left at a T-junction takes us onto a concrete road, to turn right opposite a cottage and go through a tunnel under the railway. Emerging at a road, we turn left, turning right in 50 yards (Wp.10 125M), on the path up to the chapel. (**For short walk (b)**, park at the roadside and commence from Wp.10, as described above).

The chapel is notable for simplicity rather than richness, however, there are impressive box pews, a fine font dated 1400, and the highlight, the 1330 wall paintings. Before the days of books, church walls were covered in scenes from the bible as a means of illustrating religious teachings, although the presentation of St John the Baptist's severed head to Salome is a tad gory by today's standards!

Departing through the gate, we turn right and right again, uphill, to cross a stile and turn right.

St Hubert's Chapel Idsworth

At a field corner, we turn left following the right fence line up a tranquil valley floor, crossing a stile by a gate, and, as we approach a road, bearing right, uphill, by a fingerpost (Wp.11 144M). We pass through a bridleway gate into a wood, climbing steps and turning left onto a track, and in 110 yards climb three steps to our right by a fingerpost. The footpath winds up through the woods, as we keep ahead to T-junction by a fingerpost (Wp.12 155M). (**For short walk (b)** turn left as described above).

We turn right, following a charming tree and fern lined bridleway, with all the hallmarks of a droveway. At a T-junction, by a fingerpost (Wp.13 168M), we keep left onto a footpath, crossing a stile by a fingerpost and bearing left across a meadow, with **Compton** nestling in the valley below. Our path leads us past a fingerpost to climb a stile, as we bear right, descending to cross a stile at the valley bottom. Keeping ahead, we join a climbing farm track. At the top of the rise, by a fingerpost (Wp.14 180M), we turn left through a double steel gate on our left, immediately turning right, initially loosely following the right fence line and soon picking up the obvious diagonal path across a large arable field. We go through deer-proof gates either side of a juvenile wood, bearing half left diagonally across two arable fields, separated by a thin copse.

Emerging at a road, we cross, turning left to return to **The Coach and Horses** (Wp.1 194M). A refreshingly normal pub - no frills here - complete with a ceiling yellowed by the passage of time.

One of the prettiest villages in Hampshire, two inns, a wealth of fine old houses, and an imposing Norman church with an amazing black marble font (1150 AD). We follow the **River Meon** through the village, circling round to climb above **Vineyard Hole**, with the church tucked under the hill below. Crossing a rural landscape to **Drayton**, we take **Halnaker Lane** up to **Salt Hill**, returning on a footpath over **Small Down** with fabulous views as we descend the ridge back to **East Meon**.

Black Marble font (1150 AD)

| 3 | 3¼ H | 8.6 miles/13.8km | 370m / 370m | ↻ | 3 |

Access by car:

From the A272 west of **Petersfield**, follow the signs to 'East Meon'. There's limited parking in the village; if busy, park in the village car park, walking back to **The George Inn**.

Short Walks

(a) Follow the route to Wp.8, turn left to return to **The George Inn** through the churchyard. (3.9miles/6.3km, 1½ hours)

(b) From **The George Inn** walk up through the churchyard, bearing left up a footpath and keeping ahead over a stile by the steps to follow the route from Wp.8. (5.2 miles/8.4km. 1 hour 50 mins)

The River Meon runs through the village

From the front of **The George Inn** (Wp.1 0M), we cross the road, following the **River Meon** through this attractive village. After passing **The Izaak Walton Inn**, we turn left between thatched cottages, up a tarmac path which bears right, passing allotments, before re-joining the course of the river.

At a road we turn left, passing a cluster of thatched cottages, turning right after **Frogmore Cottage** over a stile onto a footpath (Wp.2 6M). Crossing another stile, we follow the right fence line to a field corner, continuing ahead over the meadow to cross two closely spaced stiles. We cross the odd shaped field diagonally, making for and crossing a stile by a gate in the opposite corner.

Dropping down and over a road (Wp.3 13M), we go up a wide, shady, moist sunken track, keeping ahead at a junction and passing round a half barrier up a green way. Crossing a farm track, we continue to a spacious junction of tracks, turning left (Wp.4 24M) and keeping ahead at the nearby junction with a cycle trail.

At a road, we keep right, turning left opposite the next road T-junction (Wp.5 34M), up the right side of a gravel drive in front of a double garage. Passing through a bridleway gate, we gently climb, going through another gate to join a steeply rising farm track up through a wood. Emerging at a T-junction, we turn left, soon bearing right at a triangular junction, up a farm track between fields.

Turning left at the next T-junction (Wp.6 51M), we follow the main track, turning right, and then left to crest the hill, with fine views opening out. We gradually descend, passing through a gate, crossing a road (Wp.7 62M) by **Park Farm**, and climbing a stile. We turn left along the lower field edge, crossing a stile and turning right to climb steeply to the top corner, then turning left to follow the right fence line around the upper slopes of **Park Hill**. With stunning views across the valley to **Butser Hill**, over **Vineyard Hole** and across **East Meon**, we continue, dropping down the hill as our right fence turns sharply away, crossing a stile visible in the bottom corner, and descending steps to a T-junction of paths (Wp.8 85M).

For short walk (a) turn left to return to the village.

We turn right, crossing a stile onto a charming footpath, before crossing another stile and going over a meadow in the direction indicated by a fingerpost. Crossing a stile by a gate, we drop down to a road by a cottage, turning right, and in 20 yards left, over a stile by a fingerpost (Wp.9 90M). We follow the right hedge line, crossing two more stiles, on a footpath with delightful subdued rural views. Keeping ahead over a field, we cross a stile which appears in the hedge line at the far side.

Loosely following the left hedge line, we pass through a field gate and cross a stile on to a fenced path, turning left along a road by **Drayton Farm** (Wp.10 109M). After passing **Drayton Cottage** we turn right by a fingerpost, up **Halnaker Lane** (Wp.11 111M). Initially climbing, the track levels out, contouring the lower forested slopes, with pleasing glimpses of fields and valleys to our left. At a fingerpost crossroads, we keep ahead, as we are joined by the **SDW**. Crossing a road at **Coombe Cross** (Wp.12 141M), we continue along the byway, soon rising and climbing steeply.

The view from Wp.14

As the track opens and flattens towards the top, we turn left, crossing a stile by a fingerpost (Wp.13 157M). We drop down into a valley, skirting the top end of a hawthorn copse, before going up the other side, making for a field gate by a fingerpost (Wp.14 161M) which appears in the left fence as we climb. Going through the gate, we keep to the top of the ridge of **Small Down**, with quite superb views on both sides.

Passing through two more gates, we gradually descend, with the distinctive **East Meon** church below. We loosely follow the left fence line, ignoring the first field gate at the bottom corner and continuing along the lower field edge to pass through the next field gate (Wp.15 178M). Descending steeply through a copse, we cross a stile, following the right hedge line along the edge of a large arable field to a fingerpost, where we keep ahead over the right side of the summit of an arable hill. At a fingerpost by a hedge corner we turn left, following the right hedge to pass through a smart steel kissing gate.

Crossing a meadow and going through another kissing gate, passing through a small car park, we cross a road, turning right along the footway.

We follow the road down into the village, bearing right to return to **The George Inn** (Wp.1 196M) and perhaps a visit to the church.

The George Inn

A National Nature Reserve for 50 years, which despite its name, is 12 miles east of **Winchester**. It's a stunning place. From May to September a remarkable display of wild flowers, orchids, cowslips, round-headed rampion, scabious, lady's tresses, to name but a few, attracts huge numbers of butterflies and insects that forage amongst herb-rich grassland. Surmounted by an Iron Age hill fort and Bronze Age barrows, protected from excavation, its prehistoric secrets will remain locked beneath the ground in perpetuity.

Access by car:
From the A32 at **Warnford**, turn up **Hayden Lane**, following the brown sign 'Old Winchester Hill National Nature Reserve'. After 1.6 miles turn into **Old Winchester Hill** car park.

Returning to the car park entrance (Wp.1 0M), we turn left for 100 yards, and then bear right onto a path paralleling the road, with impressive views east. As our path re-joins the road we take the left fork (Wp.2 5M), the sharply descending beech tree-lined **Hayden Lane**, with fine views across to **Beacon Hill**. At a footpath fingerpost (Wp.3 23M), we turn left along a stone surfaced track, which dips before rising to pass a copse, then continues descending. A group of four buzzards with their graceful upward spiralling flight and mewing calls, was seen here in August 2005, a feathered ballet.

On reaching the bottom our track turns left to a large barn at **Lower Peake Cottage**, where we turn right by a fingerpost, crossing a footbridge and passing through an equestrian unit. Our path passes between fences to a road (Wp.4 40M), where we turn right down a lane, turning left immediately after bridge parapets (Wp.5 46M) to climb onto the old track bed of the **Meon Valley** railway. Following the old railway embankment with occasional glimpses left of **Old Winchester Hill** through the trees, we reach a post and rail fence (Wp.6 56M), where we bear left down a slope, turning sharp left at the bottom to a bridge over a stream bed (usually dry in summer).

The old railway track

Crossing, we turn left on a rising wide path, which soon turns right by a field gate to follow the left fence line round field edges, as we follow the **SDW**. The obvious path climbs the hill, and the Nature Reserve with its tree clad western slope comes into view as we turn right. As **Monarch's Way** joins from our left between fences, we pass between posts (Wp.7 73M), turning right to continue our climb, following the path between hedge and left fence line. Entering the wooded slope of the Nature Reserve, we wend our way up, to emerge through a kissing gate onto the open slopes, awash with wild flowers, the air resonating with the musical buzz of insects, and the dancing flight of swarms of butterflies.

Passing through the west entrance we enter the hill fort, keeping ahead to pass over

several round barrows at the summit, with extensive views to the **Isle of Wight** and the surrounding downland.

With a rare pond barrow on our left (the remains were buried at the bottom of the depression), we leave through the east entrance, turning left down to an English Nature information board (Wp.8 88M). We turn left down a flight of five steps to follow a magnificent path, winding across the steep hillside of the Reserve.

… a magnificent path …

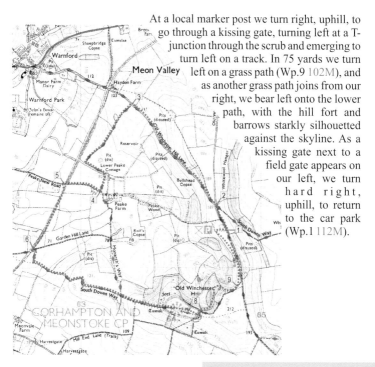

At a local marker post we turn right, uphill, to go through a kissing gate, turning left at a T-junction through the scrub and emerging to turn left on a track. In 75 yards we turn left on a grass path (Wp.9 102M), and as another grass path joins from our right, we bear left onto the lower path, with the hill fort and barrows starkly silhouetted against the skyline. As a kissing gate next to a field gate appears on our left, we turn hard right, uphill, to return to the car park (Wp.1 112M).

How our children laughed as we drove past **Cheesefoot Head**, in our old Bedford camper van, on our way to our West Country holidays! Little did I know that, years later, it would be the final walk in this book. The end of the South Downs, overlooking **Winchester**, a fine undulating walk through fields and woods, crossing **Chilcomb Ranges** and passing through the church and village before joining the **South Downs Way** for the return.

Important Note: It's <u>essential</u> to ring the Ministry of Defence on 01420 483362, 8.30 – 4.30 Monday to Friday, to check the firing ranges are not in use before setting off.

3	2H 55M · 7.2 miles/11.6km · ▲ 270m / 270m · ↻ · 0

Short Walks

(a) South section (not affected by the firing range). Follow the route to Wp.7, turn right, up the road and fork left onto the bridleway, up the ridge, to return to Wp.2. (5½ miles/8.9km 2 hours 10 mins)

(b) North section. At Wp.2 keep ahead on the bridleway descending the ridge. Keep ahead onto a road; take the next right at a bridleway/footpath junction at Wp.7. (5.3 miles/8½km 2 hours 5 mins)

Access by car:
Cheesefoot Head car park is on the A272, east of **Winchester**.

Walking back to the car park entrance (Wp.1 0M), we turn right along the verge, carefully crossing the busy road by a **SDW** fingerpost, and crossing an arable field to a fingerpost crossroads (Wp.2 4M). (**For short walk (b)** keep ahead, as above). Turning left, then left again at a corner onto a farm track, we climb a short slope before turning right at a fingerpost T-junction on a bridleway farm track.

Sunflowers for pheasants near Wp.13.

With distant views over the **Solent**, we descend to turn left at a marker post (Wp.3 16M), dropping down and turning right by another marker post on a path along the top edge of a juvenile wood. We continue down to a valley bottom, passing to the right of a small copse, and eventually entering a wooded path by a marker post.

We keep right at a T-junction on a track, turning right and immediately left at an offset crossroads (Wp.4 45M), down another woodland bridleway through a charming coppicing 'tunnel'. At a fingerpost crossroads we turn right, up a rising path, turning left at a marker post to cross a stile (Wp.5 53M). Keeping ahead across an arable field, we make for and cross a distant stile into a copse. Leaving the narrow copse over a stile, we pass along a field edge, with woodland on our left.

At the next field we bear right, diagonally crossing an arable field, making for a distant fingerpost at the corner of a wood. Keeping ahead as we join the rising track of **Old Down Lane** along the wood edge, we go over a farm road. After passing between trees and hedges and along a large field edge, we emerge at a road (Wp.6 77M) and almost immediately turn right by a fingerpost down **Old Morestead Lane**, a sunken bridleway, until we emerge at a crossroads with **Fawley Lane**, by a 'Chilcomb Ranges' warning sign (Wp.7 91M)

For short walk (a) turn right as above, **for short walk (b)** turn right onto the footpath.

Keeping ahead over the road onto the footpath, following the left hedge line, we're soon reassured by a sign 'This Footpath is not affected by the MOD Danger Zone'.

The footpath passes along the range boundary, and we always pass to the left of all warning signs as we follow finger and marker posts. So, we drop down, passing over a double stile, keeping ahead to a visible marker post at a wood edge, our route taking us up a superb rising terraced woodland path, possibly of Roman origin, as we climb parallel to the adjacent Roman road.

One of the many firing range warning signs

Our path opens out as we pass up the left side of a meadow, crossing a stile at the top up to a busy road (Wp.8 107M). Turning right, we keep close to the road edge as we carefully negotiate this fast, straight road, and in 600 yards, by a bridleway fingerpost, we turn left, crossing the road onto a bridleway (Wp.9 111M). We pass through a gate to parallel the road on an attractive path, turning right at a T-junction with a track, which brings us back to the road on a dangerous bend.

Here we have to cross, the safest bet being to turn left for 50 yards, cross, returning up the other side to pass through a bridleway gate next to a field gate (Wp.10 119M), entering the **Chilcomb Ranges** (if the red flag is flying, retrace your steps to Wp.7, turning left up the road, forking left onto the bridleway to return to Wp.2).

At the flagpole, with **Winchester** across the valley to our left, we bear half right, diagonally crossing a field on a descending grass path. Entering a wood, we follow a track traversing down the steep wooded hillside to leave the range through a gate, turning left after passing a sentry box and crossing a stile (Wp.11 129M) into **Chilcomb** churchyard.

Chilcomb Church

Passing the front door of the early Norman church, we drop down to a narrow road, turning left and downhill. As the road bends left, we turn right by a fingerpost, passing in front of houses on a gravel drive, soon becoming a grass footpath.

Near the end of the road, looking towards Cheesefoot Head car park

Turning right at a road (Wp.12 139M), we gradually climb, until, as the road turns sharply right, we turn left by a fingerpost (Wp.13 146M), up a lovely woodland footpath, crossed by the occasional deer run. Emerging, we keep ahead across a field, and over a crossroads (Wp.14 152M), as we join with the **SDW**. Our bridleway steadily climbs towards **Cheesefoot Head**, returning us to the crossroads (Wp.2 171M) where we turn left, retracing our steps to the car park (Wp.1 175M).

See the notes on GPS & Waypoints on page 17.

1

LIGHTHOUSE FAMILY

Wp	Zo	E	N
1	TV	55464	96015
2	TV	56774	95429
3	TV	57716	95316
4	TV	58837	95611
5	TV	59003	95729
6	TV	59122	95687
7	TV	59235	95639
8	TV	59444	95696
9	TV	59289	95778
10	TV	59535	96520
11	TV	59744	96711
12	TV	59393	96914
13	TV	59234	96641
14	TV	59158	96598
15	TV	58506	96148
16	TV	57578	95901
17	TV	56590	95608
18	TV	56206	95779

2

CRAPHAM DOWN

Wp	Zo	E	N
1	TV	58678	97913
2	TV	57994	97514
3	TV	57963	97209
4	TV	57740	97000
5	TV	56924	96726
6	TV	56680	97332
7	TV	56939	97520
8	TV	56579	97977
9	TV	56472	98172
10	TV	56422	98293
11	TV	56957	98740
12	TV	57403	99356
13	TV	57181	99481
14	TQ	58157	00053
15	TV	58479	98821
16	TV	58775	98262
17	TV	58836	98190
18	TV	58853	98077
19	TV	58727	97884

3

SEVEN SISTERS

Wp	Zo	E	N
1	TV	55664	97812
2	TV	55232	98131
3	TV	55117	98263
4	TV	54812	99051
5	TV	54423	98473
6	TV	53992	98691
7	TV	53759	98621
8	TV	53256	98713
9	TV	52503	98599
10	TV	52391	98883
11	TV	51973	99472
12	TV	51844	98445
13	TV	52385	97440
14	TV	53740	96848
15	TV	55230	96279
16	TV	55355	97311

4

THE LONG MAN OF WILMINGTON & BANOFEE PIE

Wp	Zo	E	N
1	TQ	55916	03799
2	TQ	55093	03987
3	TQ	54265	03551
4	TQ	53864	03605
5	TQ	54206	03276
6	TQ	54420	03331
7	TQ	54634	03166
8	TQ	55332	01903
9	TQ	55619	01846
10	TQ	56261	01399
11	TQ	56401	01334
12	TQ	57984	01738
13	TQ	57940	01902
14	TQ	57687	02272
15	TQ	56289	01733
16	TQ	56364	01936
17	TQ	56281	01991
18	TQ	56144	02500
19	TQ	56166	02570
20	TQ	56151	02893
21	TQ	56107	03172
22	TQ	56118	03352
23	TQ	56059	03506
24	TQ	56126	03637

5

LULLINGTON HEATH NATIONAL NATURE RESERVE

Wp	Zo	E	N
1	TQ	52100	03300
2	TQ	52226	03130
3	TQ	52671	03698
4	TQ	53135	03986
5	TQ	53276	04081
6	TQ	54382	04353
7	TQ	54385	04150
8	TQ	54266	03546
9	TQ	54698	03726
10	TQ	54464	03319
11	TQ	54145	02097
12	TQ	53938	01951
13	TQ	54564	01851
14	TQ	54149	00756
15	TQ	53773	00278
16	TQ	52176	00670
17	TQ	52311	01612
18	TQ	52311	01720
19	TQ	52150	01722
20	TQ	52183	03112

6

ALFRISTON & BISHOPSTONE

Wp	Zo	E	N
1	TQ	51859	03421
2	TQ	51042	03450
3	TQ	49906	04505
4	TQ	48891	02402
5	TQ	47038	01946
6	TQ	46813	01097
7	TQ	47333	00988
8	TQ	47575	01008
9	TQ	48850	02147
10	TQ	49212	02081
11	TQ	49955	02661
12	TQ	50868	02564
13	TQ	51231	02765
14	TQ	51903	02865
15	TQ	52078	03017

7

BOPEEP & THE CUCKMERE

Wp	Zo	E	N
1	TQ	49366	05069
2	TQ	48892	02398
3	TQ	49494	01529
4	TQ	51191	01439
5	TQ	52151	01726
6	TQ	52229	03118
7	TQ	51905	03495
8	TQ	51875	03795
9	TQ	51285	03818
10	TQ	50567	03966
11	TQ	49911	04508

8
FIRLE BEACON

Wp	Zo	E	N
1	TQ	46782	05858
2	TQ	45510	05970
3	TQ	45713	04797
4	TQ	46158	03582
5	TQ	46347	03106
6	TQ	46422	03155
7	TQ	48126	04308
8	TQ	48691	04721
9	TQ	49042	05363

9
BLOOMSBURY SET

Wp	Zo	E	N
1	TQ	46833	07444
2	TQ	47490	06792
3	TQ	47542	06503
4	TQ	48554	05932
5	TQ	49028	05432
6	TQ	49416	05029
7	TQ	49915	04508
8	TQ	49970	04923
9	TQ	50340	05225
10	TQ	51422	04738
11	TQ	51662	05004
12	TQ	51689	05170
13	TQ	51169	05300
14	TQ	50807	05916
15	TQ	50530	06428
16	TQ	49271	06844
17	TQ	47797	07273

10
MOUNT CABURN & SAXON DOWN

Wp	Zo	E	N
1	TQ	45807	08636
2	TQ	45633	08971
3	TQ	44536	09284
4	TQ	44339	09021
5	TQ	43964	09715
6	TQ	42619	09906
7	TQ	42333	10192
8	TQ	42404	10485
9	TQ	42805	10726
10	TQ	42831	10911
11	TQ	43884	10612
12	TQ	44587	10184
13	TQ	44592	09450
14	TQ	45532	09373

11
THREE STATIONS

Wp	Zo	E	N
1	TQ	34696	08677
2	TQ	34975	08507
3	TQ	35763	07504
4	TQ	36785	07849
5	TQ	37907	07940
6	TQ	41291	05342
7	TQ	41324	04873
8	TQ	42185	05320
9	TQ	43095	05522
10	TQ	43678	05024
11	TQ	45505	05989
12	TQ	45758	07978
13	TQ	45814	08690

12
RODMELL & VIRGINIA WOOLF

Wp	Zo	E	N
1	TQ	41842	05949
2	TQ	42099	06388
3	TQ	43194	06823
4	TQ	42749	05349
5	TQ	42193	05325
6	TQ	42126	05351
7	TQ	42064	05495
8	TQ	41338	04869
9	TQ	41290	05341
10	TQ	40762	05681
11	TQ	40614	05425
12	TQ	39344	04689
13	TQ	39599	04229
14	TQ	40753	04666

13
KINGSTON SPECTACULAR

Wp	Zo	E	N
1	TQ	39355	08284
2	TQ	38966	07986
3	TQ	38797	07843
4	TQ	38627	07875
5	TQ	38526	07655
6	TQ	37907	07940
7	TQ	36742	07383
8	TQ	36939	07253
9	TQ	36308	06394
10	TQ	37803	05851
11	TQ	37879	06177
12	TQ	38705	07521

14
WOLSTONBURY HILL

Wp	Zo	E	N
1	TQ	28102	16520
2	TQ	28914	15578
3	TQ	29323	15259
4	TQ	29417	14268
5	TQ	29097	14279
6	TQ	29064	13945
7	TQ	28464	13534
8	TQ	28511	14320
9	TQ	28577	14982
10	TQ	28322	15612
11	TQ	28107	16024
12	TQ	28245	16323

15
BATTLE OF LEWES

Wp	Zo	E	N
1	TQ	36407	13267
2	TQ	36533	13294
3	TQ	36894	13441
4	TQ	37114	13758
5	TQ	37496	13743
6	TQ	37353	13047
7	TQ	37600	12801
8	TQ	37719	12370
9	TQ	37795	12244
10	TQ	38415	11905
11	TQ	39166	11314
12	TQ	39595	11334
13	TQ	39903	11440
14	TQ	39935	11579
15	TQ	39997	12100
16	TQ	39676	11723
17	TQ	39465	11549
18	TQ	38249	12233
19	TQ	37417	12507
20	TQ	37075	12520
21	TQ	37177	12591
22	TQ	36771	12914
23	TQ	36558	13158
24	TQ	36374	13175

16
BUCKLAND BANK

Wp	Zo	E	N
1	TQ	36400	13253
2	TQ	36568	13158
3	TQ	37172	12589
4	TQ	37003	12518
5	TQ	37619	11207
6	TQ	36896	11136
7	TQ	36312	10999
8	TQ	35350	10437

9	TQ	35826	12648
10	TQ	36297	12655
11	TQ	36070	12912
12	TQ	35943	13276

17

STANMER PARK & DITCHLING BEACON

Wp	Zo	E	N
1	TQ	33664	09485
2	TQ	33456	09342
3	TQ	33189	09432
4	TQ	32830	09446
5	TQ	32528	09901
6	TQ	32326	11171
7	TQ	32661	11555
8	TQ	32845	12119
9	TQ	33041	13170
10	TQ	33378	12972
11	TQ	35241	12761
12	TQ	35113	12370
13	TQ	34974	12077
14	TQ	34339	11747
15	TQ	33742	11174
16	TQ	33690	10791
17	TQ	33648	09633

18

CHATTRI & WINDMILLS

Wp	Zo	E	N
1	TQ	30307	13434
2	TQ	30498	13240
3	TQ	31506	12889
4	TQ	33041	13169
5	TQ	32847	12115
6	TQ	31958	11726
7	TQ	31353	11585
8	TQ	31114	11744
9	TQ	30931	11762
10	TQ	30348	11083
11	TQ	30727	12105

19

DEVIL'S DYKE & CASTLE RINGS

Wp	Zo	E	N
1	TQ	24669	11338
2	TQ	24927	11093
3	TQ	25824	10945
4	TQ	26654	11502
5	TQ	26592	11724
6	TQ	26350	12007
7	TQ	26150	12350
8	TQ	25874	12349
9	TQ	24999	12434

10	TQ	24850	12518
11	TQ	24724	11440
12	TQ	24924	11432
13	TQ	24161	10914
14	TQ	23212	11002
15	TQ	23154	11444
16	TQ	23046	11946
17	TQ	23424	12108
18	TQ	24146	12049

20

THUNDERSBARROW HILL

Wp	Zo	E	N
1	TQ	20775	09675
2	TQ	22702	09141
3	TQ	22991	08330
4	TQ	23649	08510
5	TQ	23529	09335
6	TQ	23343	09864
7	TQ	23206	10999
8	TQ	23426	11396
9	TQ	23409	12066
10	TQ	23045	11943
11	TQ	22693	12603
12	TQ	22172	12887
13	TQ	21541	11543
14	TQ	21589	11131
15	TQ	21981	10944
16	TQ	21801	10625
17	TQ	21378	10409
18	TQ	20957	09958

21

BRAMBER CASTLE FAMILY WALK

Wp	Zo	E	N
1	TQ	18561	10598
2	TQ	18447	10806
3	TQ	18633	11155
4	TQ	18833	11363
5	TQ	18974	11285
6	TQ	19528	13355
7	TQ	19682	11375
8	TQ	19678	11643
9	TQ	19723	11877
10	TQ	19885	12144
11	TQ	20063	12421
12	TQ	19010	11290
13	TQ	19016	11195
14	TQ	18984	10644
15	TQ	18654	10600

22

CHANCTONBURY RING

Wp	Zo	E	N
1	TQ	14573	12468
2	TQ	13269	12470
3	TQ	12641	12212
4	TQ	12587	12098
5	TQ	13371	11958
6	TQ	14482	11340
7	TQ	16225	10005
8	TQ	16340	10296
9	TQ	16906	10690
10	TQ	16497	11066
11	TQ	16327	11022
12	TQ	16190	11219
13	TQ	16816	11708
14	TQ	16006	12038
15	TQ	15507	12174

23

CISSBURY RING

Wp	Zo	E	N
1	TQ	13300	07175
2	TQ	13822	07512
3	TQ	14263	08143
4	TQ	14005	08393
5	TQ	13939	08500
6	TQ	13812	08850
7	TQ	15117	09725
8	TQ	15147	08324
9	TQ	15708	08101
10	TQ	15994	07242
11	TQ	15793	06868
12	TQ	14981	08024
13	TQ	14352	08412
14	TQ	13503	07913

24

SULLINGTON & STORRINGTON

Wp	Zo	E	N
1	TQ	08628	14095
2	TQ	08339	14170
3	TQ	08097	14043
4	TQ	08140	13215
5	TQ	07637	12507
6	TQ	08449	12404
7	TQ	08640	12686
8	TQ	09208	12874
9	TQ	09607	12406
10	TQ	09614	11695
11	TQ	10495	11964
12	TQ	11382	12867
13	TQ	10423	12961
14	TQ	09863	13089

Wp	Zo	E	N
15	TQ	09421	13677
16	TQ	09195	13912
17	TQ	08987	14112

25

HARROW HILL & THE FAIRIES

Wp	Zo	E	N
1	TQ	08707	11958
2	TQ	08898	09772
3	TQ	08238	09306
4	TQ	08317	08225
5	TQ	08263	07785
6	TQ	07546	08134
7	TQ	06779	09231
8	TQ	06051	10182
9	TQ	06045	10938
10	TQ	07508	12382
11	TQ	08159	12238

26

RACKHAM MILL & PARHAM PARK

Wp	Zo	E	N
1	TQ	06982	12493
2	TQ	06089	12515
3	TQ	05080	12584
4	TQ	05132	13172
5	TQ	05057	13749
6	TQ	04827	13756
7	TQ	04415	13652
8	TQ	04651	14081
9	TQ	04695	14451
10	TQ	04875	14444
11	TQ	05072	14551
12	TQ	06111	14555
13	TQ	06458	14576
14	TQ	07189	14535
15	TQ	07090	13471
16	TQ	07091	12997
17	TQ	06927	12619

27

ALFRED THE GREAT & BURPHAM

Wp	Zo	E	N
1	TQ	03952	08883
2	TQ	03986	08693
3	TQ	04110	08547
4	TQ	04190	08207
5	TQ	03496	07831
6	TQ	03505	07496
7	TQ	04265	07665
8	TQ	04765	07748
9	TQ	04841	07769

Wp	Zo	E	N
10	TQ	05219	07932
11	TQ	05390	08343
12	TQ	06107	09281
13	TQ	06052	10179
14	TQ	05462	09369
15	TQ	04778	08771
16	TQ	04337	08569
17	TQ	04298	08640
18	TQ	04213	08647

28

ARUNDEL PARK & AMBERLEY

Wp	Zo	E	N
1	TQ	02522	08476
2	TQ	02354	07748
3	TQ	01864	07782
4	TQ	01307	08320
5	TQ	01154	08762
6	TQ	01221	09893
7	TQ	01271	10136
8	TQ	01472	10374
9	TQ	01916	11346
10	TQ	01847	11551
11	TQ	01707	11876
12	TQ	01816	12996
13	TQ	03175	13226
14	TQ	03194	12909
15	TQ	03420	12558
16	TQ	03787	12487
17	TQ	04456	11381
18	TQ	04410	10961
19	TQ	04056	10190
20	TQ	03862	10321
21	TQ	03102	10664
22	TQ	03333	10069
23	TQ	02835	09843
24	TQ	02592	09953
25	TQ	02591	08828

29

THE ARUN VALLEY

Wp	Zo	E	N
1	TQ	04297	18598
2	TQ	04269	18910
3	TQ	03794	18891
4	TQ	03018	18405
5	TQ	03444	17676
6	TQ	03277	17224
7	TQ	02898	16272
8	TQ	03194	15962
9	TQ	03111	15535
10	TQ	03025	15092
11	TQ	03058	13247
12	TQ	03078	12834

Wp	Zo	E	N
13	TQ	02624	11874
14	TQ	02496	11822
15	TQ	02170	11337
16	TQ	02285	10784
17	TQ	02708	10193
18	TQ	03790	08912
19	TQ	03366	08184
20	TQ	03020	07277
21	TQ	01993	06985
22	TQ	02424	06419

30

BIGOR & STANE STREET

Wp	Zo	E	N
1	SU	97353	12926
2	SU	97832	13303
3	SU	98225	14461
4	SU	98625	14398
5	SU	99425	14036
6	SU	99633	13872
7	SU	98926	13212
8	SU	98192	12225
9	SU	97385	12676
10	SU	96924	12598
11	SU	96401	11939
12	SU	96220	11700
13	SU	95161	11431
14	SU	96758	12640
15	SU	97137	12928

31

SLINDON & REWELL WOODS

Wp	Zo	E	N
1	SU	96483	08371
2	SU	96780	08538
3	SU	96905	09020
4	SU	96853	09405
5	SU	97046	10113
6	SU	97348	10276
7	SU	98166	10138
8	SU	98474	10059
9	SU	99072	09666
10	SU	99307	09437
11	SU	99953	08807
12	TQ	00604	08280
13	TQ	00564	07891
14	TQ	00595	07614
15	TQ	00142	08057
16	SU	99315	08238
17	SU	98438	08745
18	SU	97813	08012
19	SU	97228	08303
20	SU	97045	08310

32
DUNCTON & BARLAVINGTON

Wp	Zo	E	N
1	SU	95975	17016
2	SU	96022	17237
3	SU	96378	17314
4	SU	96628	17306
5	SU	96673	16451
6	SU	96781	16359
7	SU	96498	16143
8	SU	96375	15579
9	SU	96345	15227
10	SU	96238	13976
11	SU	96677	14162
12	SU	97071	14103
13	SU	97163	14169
14	SU	97612	14319
15	SU	98227	14456
16	SU	97902	15165
17	SU	97808	15311
18	SU	97300	16065
19	SU	97130	16105
20	SU	96374	16517

33
EAST DEAN

Wp	Zo	E	N
1	SU	90375	12944
2	SU	90175	12637
3	SU	89702	12154
4	SU	89666	11411
5	SU	89863	11230
6	SU	90181	10843
7	SU	90459	09984
8	SU	91316	11388
9	SU	91037	11770
10	SU	90652	12536

34
SINGLETON & LEVIN DOWN

Wp	Zo	E	N
1	SU	87763	13100
2	SU	87421	13205
3	SU	86090	14206
4	SU	87377	14990
5	SU	87497	15299
6	SU	88861	14686
7	SU	88951	14520
8	SU	88665	13334
9	SU	87987	13544

35
HEYSHOTT ESCARPMENT

Wp	Zo	E	N
1	SU	89915	18011
2	SU	90579	17441
3	SU	91258	17025
4	SU	91924	16677
5	SU	92064	16232
6	SU	90825	16441
7	SU	89955	16522
8	SU	89955	16843
9	SU	89637	16917
10	SU	89336	16508
11	SU	89166	16684
12	SU	89373	17535

36
KINGLEY VALE

Wp	Zo	E	N
1	SU	80330	11510
2	SU	79975	11831
3	SU	80067	12736
4	SU	80035	13269
5	SU	79565	13460
6	SU	79332	13571
7	SU	79013	13048
8	SU	78798	12628
9	SU	79423	11932
10	SU	79622	11602
11	SU	78906	10749
12	SU	79211	10718
13	SU	80014	10483
14	SU	80968	10341
15	SU	81894	10245
16	SU	82388	09965
17	SU	82203	10631
18	SU	82136	11092
19	SU	81888	11019
20	SU	81200	10636

37
TWO MARDENS

Wp	Zo	E	N
1	SU	80708	14607
2	SU	81402	15660
3	SU	81350	15911
4	SU	81771	15713
5	SU	82871	14435
6	SU	82843	13878
7	SU	81923	14549
8	SU	81703	14230
9	SU	80819	14458
10	SU	80669	13676
11	SU	80601	13090
12	SU	79843	13345
13	SU	79572	13944
14	SU	79704	14229

38
HARTING DOWNS & THE DEVIL'S JUMPS

Wp	Zo	E	N
1	SU	79042	18098
2	SU	80284	18539
3	SU	80998	18308
4	SU	82039	17857
5	SU	82463	18136
6	SU	82727	17290
7	SU	82456	16933
8	SU	82972	16479
9	SU	82251	16320
10	SU	81554	16212
11	SU	81407	16026
12	SU	81223	16558
13	SU	80817	16198
14	SU	80055	15908
15	SU	79706	15904
16	SU	79734	17019
17	SU	79664	17317
18	SU	79734	17393

39
EARL GODWIN'S CHAPEL & THE RED LION

Wp	Zo	E	N
1	SU	77640	14804
2	SU	77066	15269
3	SU	76466	16218
4	SU	75823	16608
5	SU	75517	16860
6	SU	74420	16479
7	SU	73758	16048
8	SU	73374	15813
9	SU	73417	14074
10	SU	74107	14037
11	SU	75146	14265
12	SU	75695	14228
13	SU	76483	13721
14	SU	76735	14213

40
EAST MEON

Wp	Zo	E	N
1	SU	68007	22158
2	SU	68444	22194
3	SU	68831	22025
4	SU	69591	22051
5	SU	69932	22828
6	SU	69303	23472
7	SU	68575	23247

Wp	Zo	E	N
8	SU	67957	22393
9	SU	67728	22577
10	SU	66966	23405
11	SU	66885	23205
12	SU	66681	21001
13	SU	67339	20159
14	SU	67527	20236
15	SU	67685	21101

41

OLD WINCHESTER HILL

Wp	Zo	E	N
1	SU	64610	21404
2	SU	64497	21674
3	SU	63563	22738
4	SU	63215	21809
5	SU	62812	21888
6	SU	62476	21219
7	SU	63445	20705
8	SU	64336	20542
9	SU	64730	20787

42

CHEESEFOOT HEAD

Wp	Zo	E	N
1	SU	52914	27726
2	SU	52730	27701
3	SU	53004	26964
4	SU	53326	25299
5	SU	52952	25332
6	SU	51449	25372
7	SU	51128	25798
8	SU	50498	26544
9	SU	50358	26866
10	SU	50218	27424
11	SU	50711	27846
12	SU	50897	28302
13	SU	51301	28065
14	SU	51655	28124

APPENDIX A
Pubs, inns, tea rooms and cafés mentioned in the text

Abergavenny Arms, Rodmell	01273 472416	Newburgh Arms, Slindon	01243 814229
Anchor Inn, Storrington	01903 742665	Old Tollgate Hotel, Bramber	01903 879494
Barley Mow, Walderton	02392 631321	Partridge Inn, Singleton	01243 811251
Beachy Head Inn	01323 728060	Plough and Harrow, Litlington	01323 870632
Black Horse, Amberley	01798 831552	Ram Inn, Firle	01273 858222
Black Rabbit, Arundel	01903 882828	Red Lion, Chalton	02392 592246
Blacksmith's Arms, Offham	01273 472971	Rose Cottage, Alciston	01323 870377
Bridge Inn, Amberley	01798 831619	Royal Oak, Hooksway	01243 535257
Castle Inn, Bramber	01903 812102	Royal Oak, Poynings	01273 857389
Coach and Horses, Compton	02392 631228	Seven Sisters Restaurant	01323 870218
Cricketer's Arms, Berwick	01323 870469	Shepherd and Dog, Fulking	01273 857382
Cricketer's, Duncton	01798 342473	Smuggler's Inn, Alfriston	01323 870241
Crown Inn, Cootham	01903 742625	Stanmer Tea Rooms	01273 604041
Eight Bells, Jevington	01323 484442	Star and Garter, East Dean (W. Sussex)	01243 811318
George and Dragon, Burpham	01903 883131	Star Inn, Alfriston	01323 870495
George and Dragon, Houghton	01798 831559	Station Café, Pulborough	01798 874546
George Inn, Alfriston	01323 870319	Sussex Ox, Milton Street	01323 870840
George Inn, East Meon	01730 823481	Tiger Inn, East Dean (E. Sussex)	01323 423209
Gun, Findon	01903 873206	Tottington Manor Bar & Restaurant	01903 815757
Half Moon, Plumpton	01273 890253	Trevor Arms, Glynde	01273 858208
Hare and Hounds, Stoughton	02392 631433	Unicorn Inn, Heyshott	01730 813486
Hungry Monk Restaurant, Jevington	01323 482178	White Hart Inn, Stopham Bridge	01798 873321
Izaak Walton, East Meon	01730 823252	White Horse Inn, Chilgrove	01243 535219
Juggs, Kingston	01273 472523	White Horse Inn, Sutton	01798 869221
Litlington Tea Gardens	01323 870222	White Horse, Steyning	01903 812347
New Moon, Storrington	01903 744773		

APPENDIX B

Recommended Things To Do

Amberley Working Museum www.amberleymuseum.co.uk

Arundel Boatyard
Hire a self-drive motorboat for a
trip up the river   01903 882609

Bignor Roman Villa   www.pyrra.demon.co.uk

Brighton Royal Pavillion   www.royalpavilion.org.uk

Charleston Farmhouse   www.charleston.org.uk

Eastbourne - seafront stroll and an afternoon cream tea at the superb **Grand Hotel**

Parham House   www.parhaminsussex.co.uk

Petworth Deer Park - a beautiful 700 acre Capability Brown park, with Britain's largest fallow deer herd. Free entry, car park north of **Petworth** on the A283.

Queen Elizabeth Country Park, a walking venue in its own right
                     www.hants.gov.uk/countryside/qecp/activities

**Weald and Downland
     Museum**   www.wealddown.co.uk

Worthing Museum   www.worthing.gov.uk/Leisure/MuseumArtGallery

APPENDIX C

Useful Web Sites

Access Land   www.countrysideaccess.gov.uk

Links to all local bus companies   www.buses.org.uk

East Sussex County Council   www.eastsussexcc.gov.uk

Hampshire County Council   www.hants.gov.uk

South Downs Virtual Information Centre   www.vic.org.uk

Sussex Archaeological Society   www.sussexpast.co.uk

Tourist Information   www.visitsoutheastengland.com

Train times   www.southernrailway.com

West Sussex County Council   www.westsussex.gov.uk

Youth Hostel Association   www.yha.org.uk

Walk!
The South Downs

with

Martin Simons

DISCOVERY WALKING GUIDES LTD

Walk! The South Downs
First Edition - January 2006
Copyright © 2006

Published by
Discovery Walking Guides Ltd
10 Tennyson Close, Northampton NN5 7HJ, England

Mapping supplied by **Global Mapping Limited**
(www.globalmapping.com)

Mapping sourced from | **OS** Ordnance Survey | This product includes mapping data licensed from **Ordnance Survey®** with the permission of the Controller of Her Majesty's Stationery Office. © Crown Copyright 2005. All rights reserved.
Licence Number 40044851

Photographs
All photographs in this book are the property of the author.
Front Cover Photographs

Looking east on Walk 38, Harting Downs & the Devil's Jumps

Cliftop route on Walk 3, Seven Sisters

The Shepherd and Dog Pub (Walk 19, Devil's Dyke and Castle Rings)

A marbled white butterfly on Walk 8, Firle Beacon

ISBN 1-904946-14-3

Text and photographs* © Martin Simons